GLOBETR

TRAVEL G

FLORIDA

LIZ BOOTH

NEW
HOLLAND

First edition published in 1997
by New Holland (Publishers) Ltd
London • Cape Town • Sydney • Singapore

24 Nutford Place
London W1H 6DQ
United Kingdom

80 McKenzie Street
Cape Town 8001
South Africa

3/2 Aquatic Drive
Frenchs Forest, NSW 2086
Australia

ISBN 1 85368 432 5

Managing Editors: Clive During, Mariëlle Renssen
Commissioning Editor: Tim Jollands
Editor: Claudia Dos Santos
Picture Researcher: Jan Croot
Design and DTP: Sonya Cupido
Cartographer: William Smuts
Compiler: Elaine Fick

Reproduction by cmyk pre-press, Cape Town
Printed and Bound in Hong Kong by South China
Printing Company (1988) Limited

Photographic Credits:
Astronaut Memorial Planetarium, p. 66; **Jon Davison**,
pp. 7, 9 (bottom), 11 (bottom), 18, 94, 95; **Chris Fairclough
Colour Library**, cover (top left), pp. 88, 93 (bottom),
106; **Henry Morrison Flagler Museum**, p. 15; **Florida
Division of Tourism**, p. 96; **Fort Myers Historical
Museum**, p. 10; **Hutchison Library/J Henderson**, p. 117;
Hutchison Library/Dr Nigel Smith, p. 12; **Hutchison
Library/Tony Souter**, pp. 49, 75; **Kravis Cultural Center**,
p. 22; **Life File/Emma Lee**, pp. 14, 20, 100, 108; **Life File/
R Williamson**, p. 116; **Museum of Man in the Sea**, p. 93;
P Murphy, pp. 13, 57, 80; **Photobank/Adrian Baker**,
cover (bottom left), pp. 4, 26, 30, 50 (Used by permission
from Disney Enterprises, Inc.), 53, 58, 59, 103 (bottom),
104; **Photobank/Peter Baker**, pp. 19, 27, 28, 29 (bottom);
Photobank/Gary Goodwin, cover (top right), pp. 46, 52;
PictureBank Photo Library Ltd, pp. 17, 35 (top), 62, 69;
Ponce Inlet Lighthouse Association, p. 73; **Marjorie
Kinnan Rawlings State Historic Site**, p. 85; **Jeroen
Snijders**, pp. 11 (top), 21, 33, 36–40, 42, 43, 67, 68, 70,
78, 81, 83, 90–92, 97, 107, 109; **Spectrum Colour Library**,
pp. 71, 115; **Travel Ink/Abbie Enock**, pp. 23, 35 (bottom),
103 (top); 118; **University of Florida**, Harn Museum of
Art, p. 84; **Visit USA Association**, pp. 25, 41; **Lawson
Wood**, pp. 9 (top), 112, 114, 119; **Zefa**, cover (bottom
right), pp. 6, 8, 16, 24, 29 (top), 54, 55, 65 (bottom), 82;
Zefa/Armstrong, title page; **Zefa/E G Carle**, p. 65 (top);
Zefa/Damm, p. 72; **Zefa/David Madison**, pp. 56, 74.

Although every effort has been made to ensure
accuracy of facts, telephone and fax numbers in this
book, the publishers will not be held responsible for
changes that occur at the time of going to press.

Cover Photographs:
Top left: *The plantation house of Eden State
Ornamental Gardens, near Fort Walton.*
Top right: *Hollywood Boulevard at Universal Studios.*
Bottom left: *Miami Beach stretches for miles and is one
of the first sights to greet visitors flying into Miami.*
Bottom right: *A space shuttle blasts into orbit in
a spectacular explosion of sound and colour.*
Title Page: *Miami, heart of the cruise-ship industry,
carries thousands of visitors to the Caribbean and beyond.*

CONTENTS

1. Introducing Florida 5
The Land 6
History in Brief 10
Government and Economy 17
The People 19

2. The Southeast 31
Miami 32
Miami Beach 34
The Everglades 36
Fort Lauderdale 38
Palm Beach County 40
Martin County 42
St Lucie County 43

**3. Orlando and
Central Florida 47**
Orlando 48
Walt Disney World 50
Around Disney 52
Around Orlando 54

4. The East Coast 63
Vero Beach 64
Melbourne 66
The Space Coast 67
Daytona Beach 71
Inland Parks 75

5. The Northeast 79
St Augustine 80
Jacksonville 82
Gainesville 84

6. The Northwest 89
Pensacola 90
Panama City 92
Tallahassee 94
South to Cedar Key 97

7. The West Coast 101
Tampa Bay
and Surrounds 102
Bradenton 106
Sarasota 107
Fort Myers 108
Around Naples 109

8. The Florida Keys 113
Key Largo 114
The Upper Keys 115
The Lower Keys 117

Travel Tips 122

Index 127

1
Introducing Florida

Flanked by the Atlantic Ocean and the Gulf of Mexico, crisscrossed by rivers and streams and dotted with lakes, Florida is dominated by water. This abundance has not only shaped the landscape, but provided a perfect playground for citizens and tourists alike.

Miami is the hub from which you can head to the spectacular wonders of **Walt Disney World**, the solitude of the **Keys** or the rolling white beaches out west. Indulge in the colonial history of the former regional capitals: **Pensacola** in the west of the state and **St Augustine** on the east coast. Today's state capital, **Tallahassee**, lies in the centre of the northern region, nominated as a compromise between feuding east and west coast settlers. Sprawling **Jacksonville** provides a gateway for travellers heading south from the eastern seaboard of the United States, and areas like **Daytona Beach** swarm with American visitors each winter.

Those in need of quiet will welcome the sunsets and the scenery. For nature lovers there is the hushed mystery of the **Everglades** and the underwater extravaganza of the **Florida Keys**. Snorkelling and diving are encouraged particularly in the **John Pennekamp Coral Reef State Park** in the Keys, and at **Peacock Springs State Recreation Area** at Luraville where certified divers can explore some of the 28,000ft (8500m) of surveyed caves.

For families Florida is hard to beat with its choice of theme parks from Walt Disney World to **Busch Gardens** and **Universal Studios**, as well as many safe beaches and a wide range of family-orientated hotels and restaurants.

TOP ATTRACTIONS

*** Walt Disney World: sensational entertainment.
*** Universal Studios: more than 40 themed rides.
*** NASA Kennedy Space Center: launch base for the space shuttles.
*** Everglades: beautiful natural wonderland.
*** South Beach Miami: vibrant Art Deco district.
*** Key West: unique island and yachting lifestyle.
*** St Augustine: wealth of history in one of the oldest cities in Florida.

Opposite: *Sailing, one of the attractions at St Pete Beach on the West Coast.*

Above: *The Everglades flow hundreds of miles, creating shady swamps that shelter alligators and other wildlife.*

THE LAND

Geologists estimate that Florida is one of the very youngest parts of the continental United States and the last land mass to have emerged from the primordial ocean. This is a low-lying region, generally less than 100ft (30m) above sea level. The highest point, at just 345ft (105m), lies in Walton County. Nowhere in Florida is more than 60 miles (100km) from a beach.

The 450,000-acre (182,112ha) **Lake Okeechobee** is the state's largest freshwater area. It feeds into the Everglade Basin, which stretches for many miles with water just a few inches deep. Strictly speaking, this is really a slow-moving river, 150 miles (240km) long and 50 miles (80km) wide. Now a protected territory, the river-cum-swamp provides a safe haven for about 300 different species of bird, some 600 kinds of fish and a number of animals, like the rare Florida panther.

To the north Florida is dominated by great **hardwood forests** and vast open tracts of beautiful beach. The **Suwannee River** flows 177 miles (283km) and is fed by more than 20 major springs before reaching the **Gulf of Mexico**. Green, rolling hills and large pine forests dominate the northwest **Panhandle**. This beautiful area, which is edged by salt marshes and expansive, sparkling-white sand beaches has been nicknamed **The Emerald Coast**.

The deep, lush tropical forests and crystal waters of the **Florida Keys** remain a haven of peace and quiet and are perfect for exciting deep-water game fishing, coral reef diving and swimming. The string of islands curves 192 miles (309km) southwest from the mainland culminating in **Loggerhead Key** in the **Dry Tortugas**, although most people consider Key West to be the end of the line.

Climate

Florida earns its epithet The Sunshine State with long hot summers, punctuated by tropical storms and often hurricanes. This area experiences more thunderstorms than any other part of the USA, the lightning causing numerous fires. Winters are short and generally warmer than in much of the United States and Europe.

The state can be divided into two climatic zones – **tropical** to the south of a line from Bradenton to Vero Beach and **subtropical** to the north. Average annual summer **temperatures** are 26.9°C (80.5°F) in the northern, and 55.1°C (82.7°F) in the southern regions. These fall each winter to about 11.7°C (53°F) in the north and 20.3°C (68.5°F) in the south.

There are however notable exceptions. Winter tourists are sometimes dismayed at the sight of **frost** as far south as Miami, though this phenomenon is rare and usually occurs in conjunction with blizzards or extremely low temperatures on the northeastern seaboard. The Keys have never experienced frost.

The summer months often bring **tropical storms** and the state averages 53in (135cm) of rain a year. This varies from about 40in (100cm) in Key West to 62in (157cm) in West Palm Beach. **Hurricanes** can occur from June to November but are most likely in September. Their movements are constantly monitored and the state has an established evacuation programme and safety procedures. Hurricanes can hit anywhere along the coast, though the worst is usually over within 24 hours, with bad weather surrounding the main storm for several days afterwards.

HURRICANES

Florida lies in the hurricane belt and the old warning is:
June – too soon
July – stand by
August – look out you must
September – remember
October – all over
Hurricane Andrew was the last major hurricane to hit this region. The storm devastated the Bahamas and reached southern Florida on 24 August 1992. It left 38 people dead and some 175,000 homeless.

Below: *Miles of white sand beaches, like Bahia Honda, line Florida's coast.*

COMPARATIVE CLIMATE CHART	MIAMI				ORLANDO				PENSACOLA			
	WIN	SPR	SUM	AUT	WIN	SPR	SUM	AUT	WIN	SPR	SUM	AUT
	JAN	APR	JULY	OCT	JAN	APR	JULY	OCT	JAN	APR	JULY	OCT
AVERAGE TEMP. °F	67	75	82	79	49	63	75	67	53	67	81	70
AVERAGE TEMP. °C	15	20	24	22	8	17	23	19	12	20	27	21
RAINFALL in	2	3	6	7	2	2	8	3	4.5	4.5	7	4
RAINFALL mm	51	76	152	179	53	55	197	71	109	109	177	99
HOURS OF SUN	12	13	14	12	12	13	14	12	12	13	14	12
DAYS OF RAIN	7	8	12	13	7	7	14	9	9	9	12	9

MANGROVE FORESTS

Florida is home to the red, white, black and buttonwood mangroves.
Red mangroves: found nearest the ocean, they survive by supporting themselves on prop roots that arch deep into the ground. They provide vital nursery grounds for young reptiles, fish and birds.
White mangroves: prefer higher ground and grow further inland, often forming hummocks with larger land-based trees such as mahogany and gumbo-limbo.
Black mangroves: identified by the short, finger-like roots that are used as airways and burst out of the ground all around the tree.
Buttonwood mangroves: are very similar to the white mangroves, also preferring higher ground.

Plant Life

Florida's sandy loam and peat ground are just two of 300 local soil types, making this one of the most fertile areas in the United States. The state is home to over 300 tree species and more than 3500 other plants. **Mangrove**, **cypress**, **palm**, **pine** and **oak** are predominant. Species like **maple** and **magnolia** are found mainly in the north.

Vast **grasslands** are found across the state, forming large, lush prairies which sustain vast herds of cattle. A unique **scrubland** covers much of the dry, sandy coasts. The freshwater and coastal **swamps** abound with trees, grasses and flowers, which provide a rich breeding ground for wildlife.

Florida is home to three diverse national forests: **Apalachicola** (hardwood/pine as well as carnivorous plants), **Osceola** (cypress swamps) and **Ocala** (desert scrub), which combined cover more than 1,000,000 acres (404,695ha) yet would all fit inside the sweeping expanse of the **Everglades National Park**. The state also offers some unusual marine parks, including the 175,000-acre (70,821ha) **Biscayne National Park** southeast of Miami

which is renowned for its many shipwrecks (some dating back to the pirate days of the 16th century) the **John Pennekamp Coral Reef State Park** around Key Largo which offers divers a close-up view of living reefs, and the wildlife sanctuary **Dry Tortugas**, west of Key West. In total the state maintains some 110 parks.

Only some 40% of the land is used for agriculture, with one-third of that set aside for timber or pasture. The farmland, however, is very productive and Florida is known for its **citrus groves**, which produce about three-quarters of all the fruit sold in the entire United States. The state is second only to California in terms of vegetable production.

Wildlife

While probably most famous for its 'gators', Florida also has many crocodiles, more than 400 types of **bird**, some 100 different species of mammal, and over 700 varieties of fish. **Panthers**, sadly, are on the endangered list, which also includes puma, boar and black bears; but

rehabilitation programmes underway at national parks throughout the state are proving successful in halting the decline of Florida's interesting fauna.

Out at sea there is a variety of dolphins and porpoises as well as the **manatee**, or sea-cow. Manatees, once hunted to the brink of extinction for their meat, hide and oil, are now the object of a dedicated protection programme.

The world of **fish** is fascinating, yielding more kinds here than anywhere else in the world, from grouper, snapper and flounder to tarpon, marlin and shark. Fishing is permitted in 35 of the Florida State Parks.

Swimming in the Everglades is not recommended due to a large population of deceptively docile **alligators** and **crocodiles**. Many golf courses sport alligator warning signs at their water hazards.

Florida's climate is also enjoyed by some 40 species of snake, including venomous varieties such as two kinds of **rattlesnake** and the **copperhead**. The **coral snake** and the water- or **cottonmouth moccasin** are potentially lethal, but you are more likely to encounter them behind glass in wildlife parks than slithering around outdoors.

More than 400 species of bird either live in or migrate to Florida – the coastal areas often form breeding sites for thousands of seabirds. **Bald eagles** and **turkeys** can sometimes be spotted inland and Florida houses the largest breeding colonies of egrets, herons, ibises and pelicans north of the Caribbean. In the Everglades you may be lucky enough to spot the rare **purple gallinule**.

Above: *Manatees were thought to be mermaids by the sailors of earlier centuries.*
Opposite: *Florida's citrus fruit is the agricultural mainstay of the region.*
Below: *The beautiful and rare purple gallinule.*

TRAIL ETIQUETTE

- Carry away all your rubbish.
- Don't feed the animals!
- Stay on designated trails.
- Extinguish all camp fires (where permitted) after use.
- Don't bring pets into parks.
- Beware of hunting seasons.
- Avoid shining torches at nesting turtles.

HISTORY IN BRIEF
Native Americans

The earliest inhabitants, native Americans travelling from the frigid north, discovered balmy Florida about 12,000 years ago. Awaiting them was a land of plenty teeming with wildlife and fish. Little evidence has been found to suggest that they were more than **hunter-gatherers**.

Primitive irrigation ditches indicate that the first farming communities existed around 500BC, although their southern Florida counterparts remained hunter-gatherers until the arrival of the Europeans. Unfortunately, many of the priceless ancient burial mounds and artefacts have been destroyed in the continuous quest for modern housing and development.

European Settlers

Florida first appears on a crude Spanish map of 1502 and a few years later was described as the 'Land of Eternal Youth' by European explorers. But it was Spaniard **Juan Ponce de León** who really discovered Florida for the Europeans in 1513. Travelling north from the established Puerto Rico, he was searching for the mythical **Fountain**

JUAN PONCE DE LEÓN

Juan Ponce de León landed in 1513 somewhere between the St Johns River and St Augustine, after mistaking the land for the Bahamas. He then sailed south around the coast, before returning to the Caribbean where he was governor of Puerto Rico. However, Juan Ponce de León was a man with a mission. He had been entrusted by the King of Spain to find the isle of Bimini, home of the fabled Fountain of Eternal Youth, and to search for gold. Having failed to find gold in Puerto Rico, stories of untold wealth lured him north. His life's mission came to an abrupt end during a later stay in Florida when he was severely wounded by a Calusa Indian arrow and taken back to Puerto Rico, where he died.

of Youth. Juan Ponce de León waded ashore on the northeast coast, somewhere near today's St Augustine, and named the land '**La Florida**' in honour of the Spanish Easter Festival of Flowers, *Pascua Florida,* that had just been celebrated aboard his ship.

Believing Florida to be no more than an island in the Bahamas, it was a further eight years before he returned to establish a colony in the Fort Myers area. But he and his men were then savagely attacked by hostile Calusa Indians. The opinion today is that the Calusas had been forewarned by their island cousins from Puerto Rico and Haiti, who had been subjected to hardship and slavery by the Spanish overlords. De León was wounded and fled back to Cuba where he died.

The next European foray into the region occurred seven years later in 1528. Lured by tales of untold treasure, another Spaniard, **Panfilo de Narváez**, landed at Tampa Bay with over 400 men. His plan was to discover how Florida connected to Mexico, but the expedition took its toll and a further eight years went by before just four of the original party managed to find their way there.

In 1559 **Tristan de Luna y Arellano** founded a colony in Pensacola Bay with 1400 pioneers; it failed two years later when the settlement was destroyed by a hurricane. However, it was revived 139 years later and on the strength of this argument the people of today's Pensacola claim to live in Florida's oldest town – a fact hotly disputed by the residents of St Augustine where a colony was established in 1565 by **Pedro Menéndez de Avilés**. He used this new town as a base from which to attack Fort Caroline, which had been set up by the French Huguenots and was seen as a threat to Spanish shipping lanes.

Above: *Pedro Menéndez de Avilés was one of the first Europeans to set foot in Florida.*
Opposite: *Calusa Indians at the time of arrival of the European explorers.*
Below: *This lovely 12th-century monastery was transported from Spain and reconstructed in Florida.*

HISTORICAL CALENDAR

1497 Europeans see Florida for the first time and record it on maps.

1513 Juan Ponce de León wades ashore and names the land 'La Florida' after the Spanish Festival of Flowers.

1559 Tristan de Luna lands and settles at Pensacola, but is forced to withdraw two years later after a devastating hurricane.

1565 Pedro Menéndez de Avilés founds the first settlement at St Augustine for Spanish King Philip II.

1763 After a century of raids by native Americans, French and British, the Spanish relinquish Florida to England in exchange for Havana, Cuba.

1783 British cede Florida back to the Spanish.

1785 The start of three years' skirmishing between Spanish and American forces.

1813–18 General Andrew Jackson enters western Florida to campaign against native Americans in three wars.

17 July 1821 General Jackson receives Florida for the United States from the Spanish in a ceremony in Pensacola.

1822 A Florida government is established under Governor William Duval.

1836 The St Joseph to Lake Wimico rail track is the very first line to operate in the state of Florida.

1842 The Second Seminole War ends with the transfer of nearly 4000 Seminole Indians to Arkansas and Oklahoma.

1845 Florida officially becomes the 27th state of the United States with William D Moseley as governor.

1855–58 The third and final Seminole Indian war takes place.

1894 Henry Flagler completes railroad as far as Palm Beach.

1911 The first night flight in aviation history is made by Lincoln Beachey over Tampa.

1958 NASA, the National Aeronautics and Space Administration, starts work at Cape Canaveral.

16 July 1969 The historic Apollo 11 mission lifts off from Cape Kennedy to carry the first men to the moon.

1 October 1971 Walt Disney World opens the Magic Kingdom in Orlando.

1981 The first manned space shuttle is launched from John F Kennedy Space Center.

24 August 1992 Hurricane Andrew hits the east coast with brutal force, destroying much of Homestead and South Dade County and causing the evacuation of thousands of residents.

Spanish Dominance

The Spanish retained control of Florida over almost two centuries despite constant warring with local Indians, the French from the Louisiana area and the British living in Carolina and Georgia. Towns were often under siege, and

St Augustine endured a 52-day attack on one occasion. Even **Sir Francis Drake** made his bid for Florida with a failed attack in 1586.

In 1763 the British forces gained control of Florida in a swap for Havana, Cuba, as part of the **Treaty of Paris**, the final settlement of the Seven Year War which had devastated Europe.

This ended military rule, with the army exchanged for civil servants. However, Florida did not remain British for long. It was used as a base against the colonists in the **American War of Independence**. After losing their battle, the British handed Florida back to Spain in return for the Bahamas.

United States Control and the Seminole Wars

The new Americans and the Spanish Floridians constantly battled over the border. By this time the population of Florida included Africans, West Indians, Greeks, Germans and Sicilians among others. **General Andrew Jackson** from Tennessee finally swayed the balance by capturing Pensacola which led to Spain's cession of Florida to the United States on 17 July 1821.

By this time the various native American tribes were collectively known as the **Seminoles**, from *se-mi-no-lee* (a Creek word meaning 'runaway'). The reluctant Indians were hustled out of their territories and despatched unceremoniously; many fled and sought refuge in the forests and swamps, hence their name. The **First Seminole War** took place during 1817–18. A second war followed between 1835–42, culminating in the Removal Act which resulted in most of the Seminole Indians being sent off to Arkansas and Oklahoma.

Tallahassee, originally a native American village, was made the territory capital in 1824 to end arguments between Pensacola and St Augustine over which had the right to lead the region. Indians were not the only problem facing the settlers. St Joseph was a boom town in 1835, competing with nearby Apalachicola as a trading port. But the flourishing community of some 12,000 people vanished within nine years, the result of a deadly outbreak of yellow fever and a destructive hurricane.

Above: *Floridians are proud of their history and love to re-enact the past. Here a man is dressed like a 17th-century soldier at Castillo de San Marcos.*
Opposite: *Castillo de San Marcos, a 17th-century Spanish castle and now one of the top attractions in St Augustine.*

Right: *Florida's citrus fruit is exported all over the world.*

Opposite: *Railroad king, Henry M Flagler, brought the first railway lines down to Miami and transformed the region.*

During the epidemic Apalachicola fared better, with some help from bank director and postmaster **John Gorrie** who was also a doctor. He treated his yellow fever sufferers by cooling their rooms, as it was believed at the time that malaria and other tropical diseases were caused by the hot sticky air of the swamps. John Gorrie did not live to see the eventual fruits of his research. Ridiculed in New York, he died a broken man survived by his invention: the forerunner of the fridge and of the air conditioner.

Florida became an American state in 1845 by which time only a few hundred Seminoles were left. A third and final war, sparked off by an unfortunate misunderstanding, erupted between 1855–58, leading to great loss of life before the proud native Americans finally had to concede defeat. A small number still live in the Everglades and their homes and villages have become popular tourist attractions.

Civil War

The battles of the **American Civil War** largely passed Florida by, although the state did supply the Confederate South with salt, beef and bacon and 15,000 troops. 1290 men joined the Union Army (the Yankee North) which captured several of Florida's seaports. Pensacola was one such city with the **Yankees** holding Fort Pickens and the **Confederacy** in control of Fort McRee. The southern rebels were the first to crack, fleeing the city in 1862. Fort Pickens escaped civil war skirmishes and became the area's first tourist attraction when the government imprisoned **Chief Geronimo** here in 1886. Crowds used to gather outside to see the Apache Indian in captivity.

Railroad

The American railroad, which was having such an impact across the country, also affected Florida. The Tallahassee to St Marks railroad, conceived and financed by wealthy entrepreneurs from northern Florida who gradually opened up the southern end of the state – helped by the enthusiasm of existing residents – operated from 1837–84. Miami was first developed in the 1860s and 1870s but it was not until 1894, when local resident **Julia Tuttle** sent a fresh orange blossom north to railroad magnate **Henry M Flagler** in frosty Palm Beach to persuade him to bring the track all the way south, that things really started to happen.

Henry Flagler extended the Florida East Coast Railway down through the Florida Keys in 1912. Although the track was destroyed by the hurricane of 1935, the same path was followed during construction of the existing Overseas Highway.

The start of the tourist trade and the expansion of agriculture both date back to the railroad development of the late 1800s. Now, for the first time farmers could export their goods nationwide and visitors could take advantage of Florida's warm winters.

Booming Miami

The original 'jetsetters' discovered Miami and the wonderful south early in the 20th century and a property boom followed (in the year 1925 alone, 481 hotels and apartments rose in Miami Beach). Devastating hurricanes in 1926 and 1935 failed to stop the flow of money into the

Below: *A space shuttle blasts off from the John F Kennedy Space Center.*

fledgling city and various events shaped and moulded its ambience. The famous Art Deco area of Miami was developed in 1930, while 1950 saw the arrival of **Cubans** fleeing the revolutionary Fidel Castro.

Most of the Cuban refugees lived in temporary ghettos, but the failure of the 'Bay of Pigs' invasion of 1961 and the threatening Cuban Missile Crisis of 1962 convinced the growing exile community that it would be a long time before they could return home. With time they came to lend a strong new Latin-American flavour to Miami, now often considered the financial capital of the Caribbean and a place where English may appear to be a second language.

Modern-day Florida

Further north the government was investing in outer space and the National Aeronautics and Space Administration (**NASA**) began operations at Cape Canaveral. The historic Apollo 11 mission was launched here on 16 July 1969, taking the first men to the moon. Twelve years later the first space shuttle lifted off from the **John F Kennedy Space Center**.

The state has continued to develop rapidly and although recession has slowed the property boom, thousands of older people still choose to make Florida their retirement home; jointly, tourism and agriculture remain its most valuable industries. By 1992 the population of Florida had grown to 13.4 million, making the state the fourth most populated in the United States after California, New York and Texas.

But the influx of people has a downside too since many of the refugees, now especially from Haiti, are poorly educated and unskilled, thereby placing enormous strain on the social aid institutions.

GOVERNMENT AND ECONOMY

The state government was formally established in 1885, although it has been modified frequently since then. The most recent changes occurred in 1968 when the electorate approved 20 revisions to the constitution.

Florida is ruled by a **governor** and **lieutenant governor** (these two candidates run as a team during elections), as well as six **cabinet members** – a secretary of state, attorney general, treasurer, comptroller and commissioners of education and agriculture. They hold office for four years, but can only serve two consecutive terms.

The Executive is supported by a **Senate** of 40 and the **House of Representatives** with 120 members. Florida tends to be dominated by the **Democrats** in both its state legislature and those serving in the **United States Congress**. Conversely, Floridians tend to vote Republican for their governors and in presidential elections.

Florida has a number of constitutional prohibitions and **tax** exemptions. There is no personal income tax or inheritance tax on homesteads; instead the state relies on corporate tax and a general 'sales and use' tax, which accounts for over half of the revenue. Lottery and taxes on special items help boost the government coffers.

Economic Development

Throughout the 1800s Florida's rapid economic development mirrored the expansion of the railroad system. Until 1821 the entire region was little more than an unexploited backwater, but, once America took control, the railroad magnates began to look further south, thereby prompting industrial growth.

TIME TO CHANGE

Florida has two time zones – Eastern Standard and Central Standard Time. The state is located in the mid-west rather than the east but such was the power of the railroad magnates, that it was included in Eastern Standard Time in order to make the rail timetables more convenient. Eastern Standard Time is five hours behind Greenwich Mean Time, while the area to the west of the Apalachicola River is on Central Standard Time, six hours behind GMT. The United States has instituted Daylight Saving in the summer, bringing clocks forward by one hour.

Below: *Florida is governed from the Senate House in Tallahassee.*

Above: *Miami has become the regional hub for cruises throughout the Caribbean.*

The original industries, **agriculture** and **tourism**, still dominate. Even today, enduring development and success depends heavily on a reliable transport network. Railroads continue to play an important part, though air travel has improved east–west links like those from Miami to Tampa.

Miami International Airport is a major hub for the region, serving not only Europe but the Caribbean and Latin America, while Orlando is developing its international links, particularly in the charter market.

Roads play an even greater role and a network of highways links most of the major centres. The **Overseas Highway** is the main access route into the Florida Keys for most tourist traffic.

With so much coastline, **shipping** is vital and the state boasts eight deep-water ports and more than 994 miles (1600km) of navigable waterways.

Tourism and Agriculture

Tourism is the state's largest industry and, despite a dip in the 1994 figures, has been growing steadily. In 1995 Florida was inundated by some 41 million visitors. About 83% of visitors are United States citizens, with most international holiday-makers hailing from Canada, the UK and Germany. Tourism is worth a whopping US$87.7 million and capable of generating in excess of US$2 billion in taxes per annum.

Florida provides the United States with 75% of its **citrus fruit** and is second only to California in vegetable production, with **tomatoes** the leading crop. The state also provides about 40% of the nation's **sugar cane**, as well as greenhouse and foliage plants. **Timber** is harvested in the north while the southern and central grasslands sustain the state's livestock and thoroughbred racehorses.

STATE SYMBOLS

Flag: White, with the state seal in the centre and red bars extending to each of the corners.
Nickname: Sunshine State.
Song: 'Old Folks at Home' (subtitle 'Suwanee River') by Stephen Foster.
Mammal: Manatee and dolphin.
Bird: Mockingbird.
Fish: Largemouth bass and Atlantic sailfish.
Shell: Horse Conch.
Tree: Sabal palm.
Flower: Orange blossom.

THE PEOPLE

Despite a comparatively slow start, Florida's population boomed during the 20th century and is today the fourth largest in the United States with some 13.4 million residents. People are concentrated mainly in the **urban belts** with vast areas of the state relatively untouched.

Floridians represent a rich cultural mix of racial and ethnic groups, each lending their special character, colour and spirit. The official language is English, though in some sections of Miami Spanish prevails. Place names have been influenced by both the original native American inhabitants and the Spanish.

Native Americans

The arrival of Europeans during the 16th century left the native American population decimated by disease, slavers, land disputes and wars. By the time the United States gained control, only some 5000 **Seminoles** remained – three wars had sealed the fate of an entire tribe. Many were relocated to Arkansas and Oklahoma; a final 150 fled deep into the Everglades, eking out an existence with fishing and hunting while modern development changed their ancestral land.

The past few years have seen a change in attitude towards native Americans, who at last have been accorded the deserved respect. Today the descendants of the Seminoles live in three **reservations** in southern Florida (Big Cypress, Miccosukee and Seminole Indian Reserve); here they use their knowledge of the Glades as a way of earning money. You can take a trip into the swamps accompanied by a Seminole guide and experience a fascinating glimpse of Indian life in one of the nearby villages, where traditional craftwork is continued and gripping dances are put on for the benefit of visitors.

STEAMING AHEAD

Florida is racing to be the first state with high-speed rail links, leaving behind the leisurely 79mph (125kph) speed limit applicable elsewhere in the United States. The service will commence between Orlando and Miami in 2004, with trains thundering along at up to 220mph (325kph). A second train will provide east–west links, travelling between Orlando and Tampa. Two of the stations will be located at Orlando and Miami airports to provide inter-Florida links for international arrivals.

Below: *A native American guide navigates an airboat tour through the Everglades.*

TOURISM

Over 41 million tourists visited Florida in 1995, a figure that increased by an estimated 5% in 1996. More than 80% of all visitors come from other parts of the United States, some 2.5 million from Canada and a further one million from the UK.
The tourism industry employs more than 650,000 Floridians and earns in excess of US$5.5 million a day.
A crime wave caused a sharp decline in visitor numbers during 1994, but concerned authorities were quick to adopt resolute action and as a result tourists were back a year later.

Below: *Tourists flock to admire the view from Sunset Pier, Key West.*
Opposite: *Cubans started arriving in Florida in the 1950s after Fidel Castro's revolution.*

The Seminoles are a proud people coming to terms with past injustices, poverty and hardship, in an effort to reclaim their rightful place in modern Florida without losing touch with their ancient heritage and customs.

The Blacks

After the United States won control of Florida in1821, white planters began to develop massive plantations, relying on slave labour. Large numbers of Africans were forcibly shipped in to man these new plantations and citrus groves, and by the 1830s the white and black communities were of approximately equal size, numbering some 11,000 each. This balance continued right up until the abolition of slavery – a federal census of 1860 found 62,000 black slaves within a population of 140,000. Although sparsely populated southern parts of Florida offered refuge for runaway slaves, northern Florida remained for a long time the deepest of the Deep South, both socially and politically. Slavery was, in principle, ended by the Civil War, but the agricultural patterns of Florida stayed ingrained for another fifty years.

Eventually the arrival of tourism offered opportunities for Blacks, though it was not until the 1964 Civil Rights Act that wider based civil liberty could be guaranteed. Today, Black people form a smaller proportion of the population than before, outnumbered by the influx of white migrants that has taken place since the 1900s.

Pensioners

Florida's demographic statistics changed dramatically with the arrival of the 'blue-rinse brigade' in the early 20th century. Numbers of white residents climbed rapidly as retirees from the northern states recognized that Florida winters were much kinder on old bones. Now every year thousands

of pensioners choose to retire in the sun and come
to Florida. This has created an imbalance and in
some areas pensioners clearly outnumber the
younger set. Plush retirement homes line choice
beaches, and many shows and restaurants cater
exclusively for the over-60's.

The Cubans

The 1950s and 60s brought a wave of immigrants
to Florida. Cubans, fleeing a harsh regime,
arrived in Key West in their thousands aboard
the most makeshift vessels. By 1980 **Little
Havana**, once the Miami ghetto area for new
arrivals, had gained solid status with undeniable
sociopolitical and economic power.

Forty years on many of the initial exiles still
harbour dreams of returning home, even as more
refugees continue to arrive. A recent new influx
occurred as tensions mounted between President
Bill Clinton and **Fidel Castro**.

Most Cubans live in and around the Miami area, con-
tributing to the tangible Spanish feel of a city where
English often seems to be a second language. Yet the
Jewish community of Dade County successfully vetoed
a move to have Miami declared officially bilingual. At
carnival time, Calle Ocho in downtown Miami comes
alive to the throbbing sounds of Cuban music, the
fragrant smell of Cuban cigars and the exuberant,
vivid colours of the costumes.

Art and Culture

Although the state of Florida is little over 170 years old it
has a remarkable diversity of art and culture. Much of its
history is on display and a willingness to preserve the past
has ensured that attractions are easily accessible to visitors.

Sarasota has become the nerve centre of Florida's
traditional arts. This central western town was home
to the flamboyant circus master **John Ringling**, who lovingly built a 30-room Venetian-style mansion as a gift
for his wife before splashing out another fortune on the

PUBLIC HOLIDAYS

1 January • New Year's Day
15 January •
Martin Luther King's Birthday
3rd Monday in February •
President's Birthday
Last Monday in May •
Memorial Day
4 July • Independence Day
1st Monday in September •
Labor Day
2nd Monday in October •
Columbus Day
11 November •
Veteran's Day
Last Thursday in November •
Thanksgiving Day
25 December •
Christmas Day
Americans generally have
less holiday than Europeans,
with only a day off at
Christmas and Easter.
October 31 (**Halloween**)
is almost a holiday, with kids
'trick or treating', nowadays
usually by car for safety.

**John and Mable Ring-
ling Museum of Art**,
which now contains the
world's finest collection
of works by Flemish artist
Rubens, and again on the
Circus Museum, filled
with memorabilia from
The Greatest Show on
Earth. Don't miss the
state's only 18th-century
Italian theatre, the **Asolo
Theater,** and its Center

Above: *Florida prides itself
on its arts and culture. The
Kravis Cultural Center in
West Palm Beach is one of
the leading venues.*

for the Performing Arts, dismantled in Italy, and shipped
and reassembled in Florida in the 1950s.

Nearby **Tampa** has one of only four museums in the
country dedicated exclusively to African-American Art.
Alongside is an interesting Museum of Art with seven
galleries of Greek and Roman antiquities, plus the **Tampa
Bay Performing Arts Center**. Most other cities in the state
boast a harmonious variety of art and history museums as
well as some rather uncommon establishments. Be sure to
visit the Underwater Demolition Team **SEAL** (Sea, Air and
Land) **Museum** in Fort Pierce, which was a training site
for navy divers in 1943, and the **American Police Hall
of Fame** and Museum in Miami.

For historical interest the spotlight has to fall on
Pensacola and **St Augustine**, the two cities vying for the
right to the title 'Oldest in Florida'. Both boast numerous
museums with captivating exhibitions as well as lovingly
preserved historical areas to substantiate their respective
claims. Visit Seville, Palafox and the North Hill
Preservation District of Pensacola or see The Old Jail, The
Oldest House, the Oldest Store Museum and the Oldest
Wooden Schoolhouse, all in St Augustine, which also
offers a restored Spanish Quarter complete with costumed
guides and a daily re-enactment of life 400 years ago. On
the third Saturday night in June each year a torchlit pro-
cession winds its way through St Augustine's old quarter,
part of a Spanish Night Watch festival.

JEWISH MEMORIAL

The moving Holocaust
Memorial on Meridian
Avenue, Miami Beach, with
its huge bronze hand and
arm stretching heavenward,
has attracted attention from
around the world. Designed
by **Kenneth Treister** and
constructed in 1990, the
inner courtyard around the
big arm is built of Jerusalem
marble and forms part of
a lily-filled reflection pond.
Engraved on the Memorial
Wall are the names of all
those who died during the
Holocaust. There is also a stir-
ring photographic exhibition.

Left: A mural in Ybor City, the Cuban heartland on the West Coast.

Though Florida escaped most of the horrors of the Civil War, some events are remembered annually, such as the **Battle of Olustee** at which the Confederacy managed to save Tallahassee from falling into the hands of the Union forces. Each February some 2000 volunteers in full uniform relive the battle at **Lake City**. A month later the soldiers are out in force again some 62 miles (100km) to the west, to commemorate the **Battle of Natural Bridge**.

Of Florida's countless festivals the **Art Deco Weekend Festival** in Miami Beach and the **Hemingway Festival** on Key West are probably the best known. **Carnaval Miami**, held each March, is an introduction to the Hispanic culture of the city, while Jacksonville, Hollywood and Pensacola all feature large jazz festivals.

Sports

In the Sunshine State the emphasis is on outdoor life with a dazzling array of sports facilities and outdoor activities. Camping in national parks, barbecuing in the backyard and volleyball on the beach have become an integral part of Florida's culture. The sun shines year-round and almost every sport has a place on the calendar.

Traditional American sports such as **baseball** and **American football** are well represented and you'll stumble into **basketball** and **volleyball** nets and goals on almost every beach and in many parks.

BASEBALL

Major league baseball arrives in St Petersburg in 1998 when the **Tampa Bay Devil Rays** play their first season, sparking a redevelopment of downtown sporting facilities. Florida already has one major league team, the **Florida Marlins**, and each year hosts the Grapefruit League when 20 of the 28 major league teams travel to Florida for warmer weather and the start of spring training. Baseball league championships take place between April and September. Supreme importance is attached to the World Series, a play-off between the best seven teams which is held each October.

Tennis facilities still manage to outnumber golf courses, with more than 7700 around the state. These vary from a court alongside a hotel or park to upmarket Key Biscayne in Miami with its championship courts.

National football league teams include the Miami Dolphins, the Tampa Bay Buccaneers and the Jacksonville Jaguars. The **National Basketball Association** is represented by the Miami Heat and Orlando Magic teams while the **Major league baseball** teams include the Florida Marlins. **National hockey league** teams are the Florida Panthers and Tampa Bay Lightning.

Motor sport enthusiasts should head for Daytona or Sebring for the Daytona 500 and endurance racing. **Horse racing** takes place in Gulfstream Park and the Pompano Harness Track offers trotting races, including the Breeders' Crown with its US$1 million prize money.

Fishing and Watersports

Watersports are split between fresh and salt, in and on! **Fishermen** have the choice of more than 7700 lakes, covering a total of 10 acres, as well as 1350 miles (2173km) of coastline. Deep-sea and big game fishing is an exciting option and day charters are widely available.

For water lovers there is the choice between surfing at Daytona Beach, snorkelling off the Florida Keys or scuba diving in natural caves. **Sailing**, **windsurfing** and **water-skiing** are offered around the coast as well as on the

Below: *Yacht Race Week off Key West attracts hundreds of participants.*

larger lakes, while **canoeing** has become a popular holiday in its own right as visitors explore the waterways, especially in winter when there are no tropical storms and the mosquito plague is not so intense. Greater Fort Lauderdale claims to be the **yachting** capital of the world with more than 42,000 vessels registered locally.

Swimmers have an overwhelming range of stunning beaches to choose from, as well as many lakes and rivers. Note that **swimming** is not recommended in the Everglades where you may suddenly be joined by a devoted croc. Most of the beaches have lifeguards who will readily advise on safety or

Above: *Palm Beach Golf Course is one of the 1100 courses across the state.*

changing weather conditions. Fort Lauderdale has the **International Swimming Hall of Fame**, complete with training facilities for swimmers and divers.

Golf

Florida boasts over 1100 of the 14,000 golf courses in the United States. Tournaments take place throughout the year and a number of courses can be booked via tour operators before you depart from your home country.

Many courses, like the **Innisbrook Hilton** at Tarpon Springs, form part of luxury resorts; of these, the **Boca Raton Resort and Club** is rated one of the top two golfing venues in the United States. An additional hazard in Florida are the alligators – heed the warning signs – which really do live in the waterways of some of the golf courses!

Attractions

Florida could rightly claim to be the playground of the world, containing literally hundreds of theme parks and attractions. The range is broad, from quaint, old-world museums to technological marvels. Every city has its theme parks and tourist attractions but central Florida is probably the heart of the industry.

The theme park industry is so prized that the state has its own **Florida Attraction Association** providing information on 70 of the top venues. Each attraction is constantly upgraded and millions of dollars are spent on sensational new rides.

JAI ALAI

Introduced into Miami by the Cubans, this game originated in the **Basque** region of Spain. It is played in a 176ft (53m) walled court called a *fronton*. The players (*pelotaris*), wearing basket-like gloves called *cestas,* hurtle balls (*pelotas)* around the court at lightning speeds of up to 170mph (275kph) while spectators bet on the winning order. Courts exist in Fort Lauderdale, West Palm Beach, Orlando, Ocala and Daytona Beach. But the oldest *fronton*, built in 1926, is in Miami, where matches are played daily.

Above: *The spectacular water-ski display at Sea World, Orlando, is a favourite with spectators.*

WHEN TO GO

There are definitely 'in' seasons when the majority of parks are extremely crowded and there are long queues for every ride. December–February offers the best climate with lower temperatures and less chance of rain, although you must be prepared for cool evenings. Late August until just before Christmas is normally quiet. Crowds turn up at Christmas, Easter and on major holiday weekends. Europeans arrive in droves from mid-June to mid-August when the weather warms up, with average temperatures around 30°C (90°F) and afternoon thunderstorms.

Young and old want to meet Mickey Mouse – the massive **Walt Disney World** complex proved to be so successful that it spawned a veritable explosion of neighbouring parks, capable of filling a two-week holiday to capacity. The Disney park not only includes such delights as the Magic Kingdom and Epcot, but also MGM Studios, some fine hotels and five championship golf courses for tired dads.

The Attraction Association has a total of no less than 26 parks listed in central Florida, from **Adventure Island** and the lovely zoo at **Busch Gardens** in Tampa Bay to **Gatorland** and **King Henry's Feast** in Orlando. Parks range from historical **Medieval Times** to the excitement of **Wet 'n Wild**, where swimming is secondary and the Surge ride claims to be the longest and fastest water ride in the Southeast.

If you are a fan of outer space visit the fascinating **Kennedy Space Center Spaceport USA** where you'll be thrilled by movies of shuttle take-offs and landings and may even be lucky enough to witness a shuttle blasting into orbit. This is backed up by the **US Astronaut Hall of Fame** where visitors can try the full-scale orbiter mock-up, whirling centrifuge and flight simulators.

South Florida attractions are more water-orientated. The **Billie Swamp Safari** features Seminole Indian shows and tours through the swamps, **Fury Catamarans** sail daily to the reef around the Keys and the **Jungle Queen** claims 50 years of serving the best shrimp-barbecue dinners while cruising out of Miami.

The more mechanically-minded will be interested in the **Henry Morrison Flagler Museum** in Miami, which pays tribute to the admirable railroad magnate. There's also the **Miami Museum of Science and Space Transit Planetarium**, as well as the **Weeks Air Museum** which hosts spectacular air shows.

Northern Florida's attractions tend to be more historical in flavour: displays of quaint Victorian bric-a-brac and train rides through the fine old streets of St Augustine. Pensacola is home to the **National Museum of Naval Aviation** and St Augustine has the eerie **Potter's Wax Museum** where more than 170 figures are represented.

> **DISNEY TRIVIA**
>
> Walt Disney World has some 30 million visitors a year. The busiest day is usually Tuesday, with Friday and Sunday the quietest. The 43-sq-mile (111km²) area cost Walt Disney a mere US$6 million. It was the first theme park in the Orlando area and opened in 1971. The park employs more than 500 gardeners to mow 1500 acres (607ha) of lawn and tend more than a million shrubs and trees while planting two million annuals. It is also the state's single biggest employer (some 35,000 workers) and tax payer (US$23 million per annum).

Shopping

An attraction in its own right, shopping in Florida is a must for any visitor. With prices approximately a third lower than in Europe, and huge ranges of stock, it's very difficult indeed to resist the gigantic shopping malls that cater for the masses.

Below: *Shopping is not limited to factory outlets – kiosks are equally popular.*

Above: *John's Pass waterfront promises an entertaining afternoon.*

Even those with just a few hours in transit at Miami International Airport can catch a cab (taxi) to one of the nearby shopping malls to pick up a few bargains. **Westland Mall, Bayside Marketplace, Dadeland Mall** and the **Falls Shopping Center** are all within easy reach of the airport and offer a stunning variety of goods.

Shopping assumes entertainment proportions at places like the **Fort Lauderdale Swap Shop** which lures young and old with fairground rides and circus performances, and **Old Town** in Kissimmee which has an antique carousel and Ferris wheel.

Speciality shops abound, but outlet malls such as the gigantic **Sawgrass Mills Mall** outside Fort Lauderdale have become big business in the past few years, offering clothing at knock-down prices.

Food and Drink

The great attraction of eating out in Florida is the variety on offer and the cost. If you fancy a 'chilli dog' for breakfast, someone will be selling one. Equally, if you want a complete meal for less than US$5 it will be available somewhere – all you have to do is hunt it down.

Ethnic restaurants mingle with American diners, fast-food outlets and seafood eateries. As well as ensuring a delectable smorgasbord of **seafood**, Florida's extensive coastline has led to the establishment of numerous immigrant pockets in the cities specializing in their own cuisine. Miami has gained international recognition for its good **Cuban** food. *Platanitos* (plantain chips) and *tortilla de papa* (a Spanish omelette) are just two of the mouthwatering options. **Key lime pie** (which traditionally is yellow, not green, and served chilled, not frozen) is a must on many restaurant menus, each one claiming to make the best and most authentic one – try Sloppy Joe's in Key West.

CITRUS FRUITS

Polk County lies at the heart of the citrus belt thanks to its warm, sunny winters and hot summers. Lemon, lime and grapefruit are among the top crops but oranges are king, helping the state earn US$1.2 billion from its fruit annually. The first orange was thought to have been imported by the Spanish and now Florida exports a quarter of the world's orange crop. The only real threat to crops is the weather – an unexpected frost can destroy the year's harvest overnight.

Stone crabs are a south Florida delicacy, served with mayonnaise or 1000-island dressing. These particular crabs are strictly protected and may only be caught at certain times of the year once they have reached an acceptable size.

The variety of food is complemented by the variety of settings. Food courts or malls have become a fast-food alternative for those in a hurry or out shopping. You can sit at any table and buy meals from any of the surrounding food stalls, allowing your party to sample different menus in just one sitting.

Most cities have areas which appear dedicated almost exclusively to gourmet delights. Try **Ybor City** in Tampa, the **Art Deco cafés** of Miami, **Church Street Station** in Orlando or the **Intracoastal Waterway** of Fort Lauderdale.

Drinks complementing the meals are just as varied. Local **beers** include Budweiser, Miller and Michelob, while Heineken leads the imports. You will be served iced water at every meal, though mineral water counts as an extra. Most soft drinks are available, except for tonic water – instead you'll be offered soda water, which is not as bitter. Be sure to try out the fresh **juices** – orange and grapefruit are musts – the main ingredient of many a cocktail, along with rum bought in from nearby Caribbean islands.

Above: *Seafood, fresh from the ocean, is on offer in the markets.*
Below: *This shop in John's Pass is paradise for anyone with a sweet tooth.*

2
The Southeast

A hot city with a volatile Latin temperament, gleaming skyscrapers, clandestine wheeler-dealing and golden beaches packed with 'babes', is how many people picture **Miami**, capital of the Southeast.

But the *Miami Vice* image of the city is only partly accurate: it has far more to offer. The surrounding region presents vast open coastal plains, wide sunny beaches and the staggering **Everglades**. The Southeast is one of America's biggest playgrounds and visitors flock in their millions to frolic in the sun, swim in the lakes, dive among underwater corals, race yachts offshore, gamble, eat out, or simply sleep in.

Flying above **Miami International Airport** you can't fail to be impressed by the city's waterways. Cruise ships steam out of the harbour, powerboats lace the ocean with white spray and swift jet-skis roar between everything.

Despite being one of the last areas of the United States to be developed (the city only dates back a hundred years) Miami has become the region's focal point. Further up the coast millionaires in search of winter sun made their opulent homes in suburbs like **Palm Beach**, which exudes money with its polo grounds, manicured golf courses and glitzy boutiques.

Nearby **Fort Lauderdale** is a well-off, middle-class neighbourhood with a myriad channels and a bustling cruise port filled with yachts of every size. Travelling north you reach **Martin County** where state parks and towns like **Stuart**, which dates back to the 1880s, lend a nostalgic flavour of life gone by.

DON'T MISS

*** South Beach, Miami: one of the hottest places to see and be seen.
** Miami: a downtown skyline made famous by many films, and just as spectacular in real life.
*** Shopping: some of the biggest malls in the world with great prices.
** Eating out: both Miami and Fort Lauderdale pride themselves on their huge variety of venues.
*** The Everglades: natural wonderland threatened by encroaching development.

Opposite: *One of the first sights to greet tourists arriving in Miami by air.*

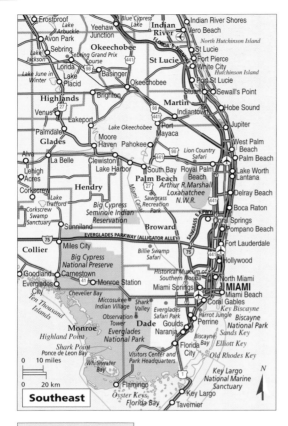

Southeast

MIAMI

Miami and Miami Beach
are actually two different
cities, each with its own
mood. Miami's mainland
metropolis was little more
than an overgrown village
until the 1890s, when one
local resident, **Julia Tuttle**,
persuaded railroad king
Henry Flagler to extend his
tracks further south. By
1896 Miami was officially a
city and by 1897 the first
tourists arrived. But those
early visionaries wanted
Miami to be more than a
mere **tourist resort** and so
started to develop its port
facilities. Today it is a major
crossroads between United
States, Caribbean and Latin
America. Exploring the
area as a whole is best done
by car, but there are alternatives, particularly in the
downtown region. Take a
Metromover (individual
motorized cars on a track)
from **College/Bayside Station** and enjoy the skyline
views. Two Metromover loops, both taking about 10 minutes, afford an excellent taste of the city atmosphere.

Downtown **

The **Bayside Marketplace**, a short walk from the station
across Biscayne Blvd, is a waterfront paradise with over
150 speciality shops, a large marina, food halls and street
entertainers. It also offers frequent free music concerts,
especially jazz and reggae. Just west of the station stands
the 55-storey **Southeast Financial Center**, the tallest

building in Florida. The Metromover takes you on to **Dade County Courthouse** (Government Center Station), once the tallest building south of Washington DC. Across the street is the **Metro–Dade Cultural Center**, a complex of water features and courtyards which houses three important buildings: the **Miami–Dade Main Library**, the

Center for Fine Arts and the **Historical Museum of Southern Florida**. The landmark **Gusman Center for the Performing Arts**, which offers numerous ballet and symphonic orchestra performances, can be found near First Street Station, on **Flagler Street**.

Above: *The Biltmore Hotel – a reminder of bygone glories.*

To explore the rest of Miami you need a car. **Coconut Grove**, first settled in 1884, was Miami's first real community. Today its emphasis is on the bohemian, and chic boutiques and elegant restaurants lie alongside tiny bars and street cafés. **CocoWalk** is at the heart, with retail and entertainment outlets in a European village-style setting. Be sure to visit the **Barnacle**, home of Miami pioneer Commodore Ralph Munroe, which contains much of its original furniture. **Charles Avenue**, the home of many Bahamian settlers who arrived in the late 1880s, retains its Victorian charm with red-brick sidewalks and ornate street lights. The pretty **Coconut Grove Playhouse** hosts Broadway plays each winter.

Coral Gables, the first planned community in the United States, was the brainchild of George Merrick. Its appeal has to do with the different 'village' designs, each representing the architectural style of a particular country or people, such as Chinese, Dutch–South African, French and Spanish. The **Biltmore Hotel**, a replica of the Giralda tower, is a classic Spanish example. Downtown Coral Gables also has its own shoppers' heaven, the **Miracle Mile**, lined with inviting shops and restaurants.

LITTLE HAVANA

Little Havana, west of the downtown area, was the first stop for Cubans fleeing their island after Fidel Castro's takeover in the 1950s. Most of the original exiles have moved on, but there is still a Caribbean vibrancy to the area which is now home to a mix of Cubans, Nicaraguans and Colombians.

The main street, Calle Ocho, is lined with coffee shops and fruit stalls. Try out specialities like plantain, rice and beans, chicken and pork, all cooked Cuban-style.

The whole place comes alive each March for the week-long Little Havana festival, Carnaval Miami. On 17 April Cubans remember those who died in the failed Bay of Pigs invasion, with a ceremony on Cuban Memorial Boulevard.

> **KEY BISCAYNE**
>
> Key Biscayne, a former coconut plantation, has remained relatively undeveloped, though affordable only to the very wealthy. It is accessible and worth a visit, as it offers one of the best beaches in Miami. **Crandon Park Beach** is rated among the top 10 in the country with its manicured grassy fringes and clean sand. **Virginia Key** to the north is site of the **Miami Seaquarium**, home of the TV star Flipper as well as Lolita, the killer whale.

MIAMI BEACH

Miami Beach relishes its reputation as one of the hottest, hippest destinations in the United States. Singer Gloria Estefan and Island Records founder, Chris Blackwell, are among the celebrities who own hotels here. Aspirant models strive to be noticed at the top clubs and restaurants, many of which are owned by the likes of actor Sean Penn, and the popstar formerly known as Prince. You'll recognize so many settings that sometimes it may seem as as though you had wandered onto a film set by mistake.

Art Deco District ★★★

Miami Beach, a collection of 17 islands in **Biscayne Bay**, was first developed by millionaire promoter Carl Graham Fisher in 1912 and has enjoyed 'boom or bust' prosperity since then. The famous **Art Deco District** along Ocean Drive was the product of a boom and now provides the setting for a 1990s revival. At the **Art Deco Welcome Center** you can obtain details of the 800 protected buildings in the area and book walking or cycling tours of the area.

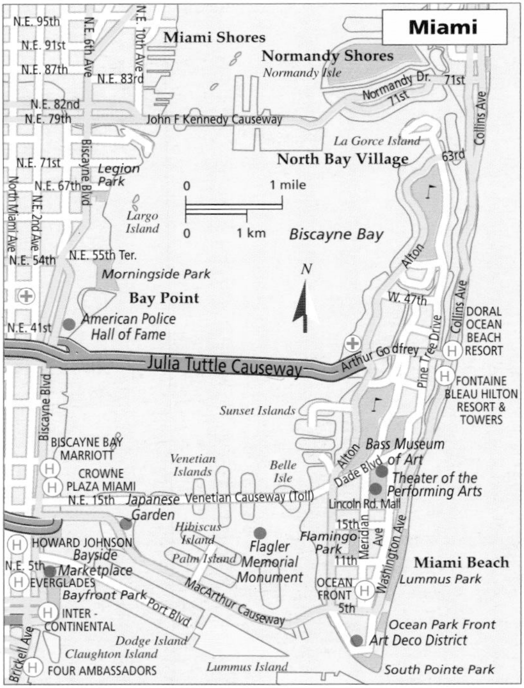

Ocean Drive has proved a sublime film setting: pastel-hued buildings, vibrant blue skies, gently swaying palm trees and the ocean beyond create a perfect backdrop. **Collins Avenue** lies a block further and is another delight of grand architecture and fading glory. The Leslie, Impala, Carlyle and Cavalier are just some of the fine hotels to admire.

Head on to **Lincoln Road** in South Miami Beach to discover the country's first pedestrian shopping mall, today enjoying a revival as an arts centre. The **Lincoln Road Colony Theater**, the **Miami City Ballet** (where you can watch rehearsals through the shopfront window) and the **South Florida Art Center** which houses artists' studios and displays should not be missed. At the southern tip of Miami Beach is **South Pointe Park** with views extending across the water to downtown Miami and east out to sea.

The Islands **★★**

Miami Beach is not just about SoBe, as South Beach is known. Check out **Watson Island**, which was created by dredging in 1931, and pay a visit to the celebrity-studded islands of **Palm, Star** and **Hibiscus**, whose residents have included Al Capone (he once lived at 93 Palm Avenue, Palm Island), film stars like Don Johnson at 8 Star Island, and Damon Runyan, whose address was 271 Hibiscus Island. Marvel at the **Japanese Garden** given to the city in 1961 by Kiyoshi Ichimura, the founder of Ricoh, where focal points are an octagonal pavilion, the Hakkaku-Do, as well as the eight-ton granite statue of *Hotei*, the smiling god of prosperity. There's also the **Bass Museum of Art** with its permanent collection of Old Masters, and the **Flagler Memorial Monument**.

Above: *Miami's Art Deco District has become a major tourist attraction.*
Below: *Miami Beach teems with visitors throughout the summer.*

You'll also want to spend time on the beach which stretches 10 miles (16km) down the coast. High-rise hotels line the beaches filled with sun-worshippers. Every available watersport can be tried out before eating or drinking in any of a countless choice of restaurants and bars.

Above: *An airboat glides through the Everglades.*

THE EVERGLADES

One of the main excursions from Miami is to the Everglades. Officially designated in 1947, the **Everglades National Park** is actually a 'river of grass' with water running just a few inches deep for over 100 miles (161km), until it empties into the Bay of Florida. This vast park covers more than a million acres (404,695ha) and stretches from east to west across southern Florida.

Habitats vary from mangrove swamp to pineland, hardwood hummocks and prairies, all home to an enormously diverse population of birds and, of course, countless alligators. Splendid orchids bloom in the Everglades, as well as some lovely bromeliads. In summer the area also spawns millions of bloodthirsty mosquitoes. The best time to visit the Everglades is in winter when mosquitoes are relatively low in number and the lack of water concentrates birds around the remaining ponds. If you do visit in summer, be sure to take plenty of insect repellent and try to keep covered up.

The disadvantage of visiting in winter are the crowds. You need to book camp sites and can expect a hum of people at the visitor centres. Unfortunately, the hordes of tourists have a potentially lethal effect on the vulnerable ecosystem of the Everglades. It is therefore advisable to stay on the paths, not to pick flowers, leave litter, or harm any animals. Experts warn that the number of migratory birds is declining and that the grass swamps are being polluted by surrounding agricultural activity. Environmentalists are finally heeding the ominous signs and are hoping to win their battle to preserve the area, but Florida's black bears and panthers have already suffered and their numbers have dwindled rapidly over the years.

For general information on the Everglades, head to the **Main Visitor Center** on State Road 9336, or the nearby **Royal Palm Visitor Center**. From here, many visitors choose to follow the 37-mile (60km) road down to **Flamingo** at the southern tip of the park, where there is another visitor centre.

The park is criss-crossed by good walking and cycling trails making the area very easy to explore. Boardwalks allow visitors to climb above the mangrove swamps for a bird's eye view of the wildlife. Trails are extremely well maintained, particularly at the **Corkscrew Swamp Sanctuary** near Naples on the western side of the park. **Canoes** are available for rent, as are **airboat tours**. Gliding across the water, like something out of a James Bond movie, these silent craft are one of the most popular ways to explore without getting your feet wet. Everglades National Park Boat Tours take visitors to the **Ten Thousand Islands** of the swamps and boast frequent sightings of manatees, ospreys and eagles.

Miccosukee Indian **guides** may be hired to lead the way to one of the abandoned, old villages deep in the Everglades, where colourful displays of tribal arts and crafts are on show.

From **Shark Valley**, one of the main entrances to the Everglades, you can take a 14-mile (20km) **tram tour** to an observation tower overlooking the Everglades, with boardwalks and hiking trails. Close by is the **Everglades Safari Park,** which presents a spine-chilling alligator wrestling show.

Below: *The Everglade swamps are a perfect habitat for alligators.*

FORT LAUDERDALE

The capital of Broward County was named after Major William Lauderdale who established a fort here in 1838, during the Seminole Indian wars. Until 1911 there were just 175 residents and it was not until the boom years of the 1920s that it became more than a dot on the map.

After 1960 this resort developed a huge following among America's students who headed to the city in their thousands for their traditional spring break. The riotous success of these holidays put off many of the more sedate tourists and eventually the city chiefs forced the students on. Today it is considered one of the top family destinations with its 23 miles (37km) of beach and average year-round temperature of 77°F (25°C).

On the Water **

No visit is complete without a ride on a water taxi down the labyrinth of channels and rivers that criss-cross the area. This is sometimes the quickest form of transport, particularly when cars are held up as bridges open to let tall ships through. Nevertheless, Fort Lauderdale is generally an accessible and safe city, considered one of the best addresses in the United States. The city is working hard to lure more visitors with new attractions, and over 2500 restaurants. Many cruise ships depart from this harbour and large numbers of people stay for at least one night.

Below: *Rollerbladers and joggers enjoy the promenade in Fort Lauderdale.*
Opposite: *Fort Lauderdale's Swimming Hall of Fame is a monument to sunshine and fine weather.*

Fort Lauderdale has some of the best shopping in Florida. Prices are generally lower than in Europe and giant malls like **Aventura, Broward,** the **Festival Flea Market** and **Galleria** make it easy to find almost anything. The **Sawgrass Mills Mall** on Sunrise Boulevard claims to be the largest shopping centre in the world with over 250 stores – free shuttles are available from downtown hotels. **Las Olas Boulevard**

is a collection of glitzy boutiques and art galleries, with street entertainment at weekends. The road ends on the Fort Lauderdale 'Strip', once a notorious student haunt, but now redeveloped with a US$26 million promenade.

Downtown **

The downtown area is relatively small and few attractions are more than 2 miles (3km) from the sea. The **Swimming Hall of Fame Museum** lies only a short walk from Las Olas Boulevard, the **Bahia Mar Resort and Yachting Center** a little further down the block. Las Olas Boulevard is also home to the **Museum of Art**, offering a collection of American and European art. Heading back down the boulevard to the mainland, you enter the residential area of **The Isles** where gardens border on canals and large yachts are moored in the backyard of almost every house.

Fort Lauderdale is very proud of its **Broward Center for the Performing Arts**, which opened in 1991 at a cost of US$52 million and is considered to be the cultural centre of south Florida. **The Museum of Discovery and Science** is essentially an interactive facility – perfect for children – but there's also the 55ft x 71ft (17m x 22m) **IMAX Theater** screen. With its state-of-the-art sound and optical equipment, the films shown here are an experience not to be missed. Nearby is **Stranahan House**, once a trading post for Seminole Indians and the home of pioneer Frank Stranahan. Nowadays it houses a museum with period furniture and art. **Bonnet House,** situated at 900 N Birch Road, is still the home of the Bartlett family who have maintained its 1920s Florida plantation-house style. The 35-acre (14ha) estate and the house are open to the public from May to November. Call for tour times on tel: (954) 563-5393.

Below: *Whitehall was railroad magnate Henry Flagler's Palm Beach home.*
Opposite: *Polo is one of the favourite sports in upmarket Palm Beach.*

PALM BEACH COUNTY

South of Palm Beach lies lovely **Boca Raton** which claims to be one of Florida's most attractive cities with its Spanish Revival style and 5 miles (8km) of glorious oceanfront. **Delray Beach**, a little further on, is worth a visit just for the Japanese Gardens and interesting Morikami Museum of Japanese Culture. The 200-acre (81ha) garden is famed for its bonsai which include the only known collection of Floridian bonsai plants. It also houses a Shinto shrine, a traditional Japanese teahouse and some picnic pavilions, as well as a recently added audiovisual exhibit about Japanese culture.

Palm Beach ★★★

Palm Beach itself was created as an exclusive resort for the rich and famous and, more than a hundred years on, has retained its distinguished air. Less than 70 miles (112km) north of Miami, it is light years away in style and atmosphere. City centre bustle is replaced by elegant calm. Like so much of southern Florida, Palm Beach owes its success to railroad king **Henry Flagler**, since it was the first town that he developed on the east coast of Florida. He was helped by architect **Addison Mizner**, who had been commissioned by some of America's wealthiest – the Vanderbilts, the Whitneys and the Wanamakers – after an enormously successful debut with the Everglades Club on Worth Avenue.

Whitehall, Henry Flagler's magnificent and imposing home, still stands on Cocoanut Row in Palm Beach and is now open as a museum filled with many original furnishings and even a private railway car. Other attractions include an impressive art collection, complete with a masterful Gainsborough, as well as a 1200-pipe organ and unusual architecture – the dining room ceiling is a stunning combination of gilded wood carving and papier-mâché. The house is open 10:00–17:00 Tuesday–Saturday; noon–17:00 Sunday. After visiting the home of the man who made the dream come true, take a trip down exclusive **Worth Avenue** and watch as millions of dollars exchange hands for top fashion, jewellery and toys.

This is also the town to catch up on your polo. There are three grounds for you to choose from and some games are free to watch. Alternatively, indulge in a round of croquet or head out to play on one of the county's 145 golf courses.

Palm Beach County offers about 47 miles (75km) of beach with excellent watersports facilities. Five species of turtle along with thousands of coral reef

fish occur along this shoreline – and, because this is Palm Beach, a 1967 Rolls Royce Silver Shadow, purposely sunken to provide an 'upmarket' dive site.

West Palm Beach *

Across the water from Palm Beach is the largest city in the county, West Palm Beach, home to the relatively new **Kravis Cultural Center** as well as the **Dreher Park Zoo** and the **Norton Gallery of Art** and **Norton Sculpture Gardens** – which are probably visited more for their botanical appeal (indigenous plants, including 300 species of palms, attract prolific birdlife). The **South Florida Science Museum** features hands-on exhibits for all ages, an aquarium and planetarium shows. It also houses southern Florida's most powerful telescope, with night-sky viewing on Fridays if the weather permits.

The **Lion Country Safari** west of town is a 500-acre (202ha) complex where lions and giraffes, elephants, antelope and zebras roam free. Ensure that you arrive early in order to beat the crowds.

POLO

Polo matches are held in West Palm Beach. Celebrities and the wealthy frequently attend to watch a *chukka* (7½ minutes of continuous play) and sip champagne. If you want to watch try:
Gulf Stream Polo Club, tel: (407) 965-2057. No admission fee for Friday and Sunday games, December–April.
Royal Palm Polo, tel: (407) 994-1876. Games played on Sundays, June–October, January–April.
Palm Beach Polo and Country Club, tel: (407) 793-1440. Host of the World Cup (April). Prince Charles used to play here.

Just down the road from the Lion Country Safari is the **Arthur R Marshall Loxahatchee National Wildlife Reserve**, which forms part of the northern Everglades. This untouched wilderness area is perfect for walking or canoeing and provides an opportunity for visitors to discover the original Florida. To get slightly closer to the animals, visit film star **Burt Reynolds' Ranch and Film Studio** at Jupiter. A working horse farm with exotic animals, its attractions include a children's farmyard where young ones are encouraged to handle the animals, as well as a round trip past several film sets.

Above: *Classic cars and baseball memorabilia fill the Elliott Museum in Stuart.* **Opposite:** *The inland parks offer a wealth of canoeing opportunities.*

MARTIN COUNTY

Travelling north from Palm Beach the slick tourist resorts dwindle into a wilderness of river swamps, mangrove forests and offshore islands. Towns are replaced by wildlife refuges and conservation areas lining Florida's largest inland waterway, Lake Okeechobee.

Stuart, the major town in Martin County, was founded in the 1880s and is a mecca for fresh- and saltwater anglers. Sights in the town include the **Elliott Museum** built by inventor Harmon Parker Elliott. Inside, a baseball hall of fame contains memorabilia of Babe Ruth and Ty Cobb, though the museum's real attraction is its treasure trove of gizmos. Elliott and his father Sterling claimed more than 200 patents, and early examples of their wizardry are on display, including an early version of an answering machine. It also houses a substantial collection of bicycles, motorcycles and cars – there's even a 1922 Rolls Royce Pall Mall Phantom. Open 13:00–16:00 daily.

Gilbert's Bar House of Refuge, named after the offshore reef that caused many shipwrecks in earlier centuries, was once a haven for shipwrecked sailors. It now houses mementos of early seafaring days.

LAKE OKEECHOBEE

Lake Okeechobee, on the western fringes of Palm Beach County, covers 448,000 acres (181,303ha). It is the fourth-largest natural lake in the United States yet is rarely more than 16ft (5m) deep. Although the lake is a mecca for fishermen, facilities for other activities are limited. **Pahokee** and **Belle Glade** have marinas and boat ramps. The lake traditionally drains into the Everglades, providing nutrient-rich waters for the swamps. Drainage for agricultural purposes has led to fierce clashes between farmers and environmentalists. Farmers need the water for their lands, while environmentalists maintain that the swamps should be left undisturbed.

Outdoors **

Almost opposite the Elliott Museum is the 40-acre (16ha) **Coastal Science Center** operated by the Florida Oceanographic Society, with interesting displays on coastal ecology as well as several nature trails.

Massive **Jonathan Dickenson State Park** covers 11,300 acres (4573ha). Visitors can roam paths leading through scrub, flatwoods, mangroves and river swamps or take a tour down Florida's only designated wild river, the Loxahatchee. Guides can be booked through the **Trapper Nelson Interpretive Site**, tel: (407) 546-2771, named after a man who lived in these wilds for almost 40 years. You can also book canoe trips, horse-riding trails and overnight cabins.

At nearby Hobe Sound, the **St Lucie Inlet State Preserve** is accessible only by private boat. A 1094yd (1000m) boardwalk takes visitors through mangrove forests out to miles of sandy beach. Each summer the area becomes home to nesting loggerhead, green and leatherback turtles, as well as a screeching profusion of seabirds. The offshore reefs are popular with snorkellers and scuba divers for their colourful corals, myriad tropical fish and, occasionally, a glimpse of a turtle.

St Lucie County

North of Stuart lies the old town of **Fort Pierce**, where you'll find the **St Lucie County Historical Museum**. It contains many early 20th-century military artefacts as well as a Spanish treasure room. But the real purpose of a visit is the **Fort Pierce Inlet State Recreation Area**. A sandy ocean floor and good Atlantic waves make this a choice surfing spot, while the windswept dunes and coastal hummocks provide an interesting nature trail.

FINDERS KEEPERS

Some 1800 ships are believed to have sunk along Florida's **Treasure Coast** during the 16th and 17th centuries. Laden **Spanish galleons** on their way from the New World back to Europe were prime targets for the British fleet and pirates alike. Vessels also fell prey to sudden, severe storms and treacherous reefs. The most famous recovery of gold and jewels occurred in 1985, when **Mel Fisher** recovered US$100 million of booty from the *Atocha* and *La Margarita*. Experts estimate that there is another US$250 million worth of sunken treasure to salvage.

The Southeast at a Glance

With temperatures rarely dropping below 60°F (16°C), southeast Florida is popular both summer and winter. In the hotter but less busy **summer** months, **tropical thunderstorms** herald the arrival of dense swarms of mosquitoes. Southern Florida lies in the **hurricane belt** and is most likely to be hit during **September/October**.

Miami International Airport, tel: (305) 876-7000, 6 miles (10km) from the downtown area, is the major gateway to the region with hundreds of flights arriving daily from Europe, the United States, the Caribbean and South America. Free **shuttle buses** run between the airport and hotels in the area. There are also **Metrobus** and **Greyhound** services from the airport. Most **car rental** firms are represented at the airport – all have greatly increased security in the wake of tourist attacks a few years ago. **Fort Lauderdale–Hollywood International Airport**, tel: (954) 359-6111, and **Palm Beach International Airport**, tel: (407) 471-7400, both offer good domestic connections. Again, hotels offer shuttle services and there are plenty of taxis. **Gray Line**, tel: (305) 561-8886, operates shared-ride and private car service.

Driving south down Florida's **Turnpike** is the best route by car. **Greyhound** has bus services into southern Florida, and **Amtrak** offers trains direct from New York as part of a national network. **Cruise ships** berth in Miami, Fort Lauderdale and Palm Beach. **Car hire** can be very good value in Florida. Rented cars are no longer identified by special number plates or stickers, since this singled out their tourist drivers, who became an easy target for crime some years ago. As in all major cities worldwide, common sense is advised, especially when travelling around unaccompanied. The **Metromover** in Miami provides good downtown transport while **Metrobuses** operate across the greater Miami area, backed by **Metrorail** operations. Fort Lauderdale's land-based transport system is supported by an extensive network of **water taxis**. **Cabs** (taxis) are easy to flag down and usually congregate around hotels.

Miami/Miami Beach
LUXURY
Marlin Hotel, 1200 Collins Avenue, Miami Beach, tel: (305) 673-8770, fax: 673-9609. Trendy hotel in the Art Deco district.
The Biltmore Hotel, 1200 Anastasia Avenue,

Coral Gables, tel: (305) 445-1926, fax: 448-9976. Elegant reminder of who Coral Gables was built for.

MID-RANGE
Miami International Airport Hotel, NW 20th Street and LeJeune Road, Concourse E, Upper level, tel: (305) 871-4100, fax: 871-0800. Inside the airport terminal, perfect for overnighting before early flights.
Holiday Inn Downtown Miami Hotel, 200 SE 2nd Avenue, tel: (305) 374-3000, fax: 374-3000, ext. 1504. Centrally located hotel.

BUDGET
Miami River Inn, 118 SW South Drive, Miami, FL33130, tel: (305) 325-0045, fax: 325-9227. Half the rooms are reserved for non-smokers.

Fort Lauderdale
LUXURY
Radisson Bahia Mar Beach Resort, 801 Seabreeze Blvd, tel: (954) 764-2233, fax: 524-6912. Across the road from the ocean.

MID-RANGE
Ocean Manor Resort Hotel, 4040 Galt Ocean Drive, tel: (954) 566-7500, fax: 564-3075. Spacious rooms with ocean or city views.

BUDGET
Travelodge, tel: (800) 578-7878. Group of low-priced

The Southeast at a Glance

hotels with nine properties around Orlando. The rates include free morning coffee, a free newspaper and free Cable TV service.

Palm Beach
LUXURY
The Breakers, One South Country Road, Palm Beach, tel: (407) 655-6611. The ultimate in glitz and glamour.

MID-RANGE
Heart of Palm, 160 Royal Palm Way, tel: (407) 655-5600. Walking distance to ocean. Value for money in an otherwise expensive town.

BUDGET
Days Inn, 2300 45th Street, West Palm Beach, tel: (800) 352-6786. Hotel chain offering basic facilities at low cost.

WHERE TO EAT

Miami
The News Cafe, 800 Ocean Drive, South Beach, tel: (305) 538-6397. Very trendy, great for people-watching.
South Beach Brasserie, 910 Lincoln Road, South Beach, tel: (305) 673-1476. Owned by Michael Caine.
La Carreta, 3632 SW Eighth Street, tel: (305) 444-7501. Cheap Cuban restaurant in the heart of Little Havana.
Lucky Cheng's, 1412 Ocean Drive, South Beach, tel: (305) 672-1505. Lively atmosphere, Asian food and lots of gender impersonators.

Fort Lauderdale
Mai-Kai, 3599 N Federal Highway, tel: (954) 563-3272. Specializes in Polynesian food.
East City Grill, 505 N Atlantic Blvd, tel: (954) 565-5569. Award-winning cuisine.

Palm Beach
The Breakers, 1 S County Road, tel: (407) 655-6611. Reservations required; dress smartly for this famous hotel.

TOURS AND EXCURSIONS

American Golf Corporation, Miami, tel: (305) 382-3935. Details of three 18-hole public courses in the Miami area.
Paddlewheel Queen, Bayside Marketplace, Miami, tel: (305) 564-7659. Cruises include meals, music, dancing and entertainment.
Everglades Holiday Park Airboat Tours, 21940 Griffin Road, Davie, tel: (305) 434-8111, 09:00–17:00 daily.
Flamingo Gardens and Arboretums, 3750 Flamingo Road, Davie, tel: (305) 473-2955, 09:00–17:00, year round. Guided tram tours through citrus groves, rainforests and hummock areas.

USEFUL CONTACTS

Tourist Offices
Miami:
701 Brickell Ave, Suite 2700, Miami, tel: (305) 539-3000, fax: 539-3113.
Fort Lauderdale:
200 E Las Olas Blvd, Suite 1500, Fort Lauderdale, tel: (954) 765-4466, fax: 765-4467.
Palm Beach: 1555 Palm Beach Lakes Blvd, Suite 204, West Palm Beach, FL 33401, tel: (407) 471-3995, fax: 471-3990.
St Lucie County:
2300 Virginia Avenue, Fort Pierce, FL 34982, tel: (407) 468-1535, fax: 467-2132.
National Hurricane Center, Coral Gables, Miami, tel: (305) 229-4404.
Arthur R Marshall Loxahatchee National Wildlife Refuge, Route 1, Palm Beach, tel: (407) 732-3684.
Everglades National Park, PO Box 279, Homestead, Fl33030, tel: (305) 247-6211.
Biscayne National Park, PO Box 1396, Homestead, FL 33090-1369, tel: (305) 247-2040.

MIAMI	J	F	M	A	M	J	J	A	S	O	N	D
AVERAGE TEMP. °F	67	68	72	75	78	81	82	83	82	79	73	68
AVERAGE TEMP. °C	15	16	18	20	22	24	24	25	24	22	19	16
HOURS OF SUN DAILY	12	12	12	13	13	14	14	14	13	12	12	12
RAINFALL in	2	2	2	3	6.5	9	6	7	8	7	2.5	2
RAINFALL mm	51	51	51	76	165	229	152	179	203	179	63	51
DAYS OF RAINFALL	7	7	7	8	12	15	12	13	14	13	8	7

3
Orlando and
Central Florida

A dream come true for young and old alike, a dazzling fantasy land where everything is fun, where happy children play and carefree adults laugh – this is the home of **Mickey Mouse**, probably the most concentrated theme park area in the world. Whether you want to watch an alligator wrestling match, hug Minnie Mouse, eat out in the Wild West, or get your adrenaline pumping on daring rides, it is all possible here.

Take your pick from the delightful splendours of the **Magic Kingdom** and educational **Epcot**, the thrills of **Universal Studios** or **Wet 'n Wild** and **Sea World**. In an area where development really started only 100 years ago, the fun doesn't stop when the sun sets.

Most theme parks are located in **Orlando** and on the road south towards **Kissimmee–St Cloud**. Increasing numbers of visitors fly straight to Orlando to start their holiday and then cherry-pick other attractions in the state.

There are some choice **hotels** inside the Walt Disney World complex, where you can share your cornflakes with Mickey Mouse; alternatively you may prefer the cheaper option and stay slightly further away.

If you need to dilute the intensity of the parks, there are several tempting options. Why not explore the elegant shops of Orlando's **Winter Park**, or nearby Kissimmee–St Cloud which retains its cowboy style of old and hosts the **Silver Spurs Rodeo** in February each year. Admire the thoroughbred racehorses of **Ocala** or frolic in the shimmering lakes of **Lake County**. And to the south lies scenic **Polk County**, fragrant heart of the citrus belt.

DON'T MISS

*** Magic Kingdom:
this is the reason most people visit Florida – the home of Mickey Mouse.
*** Universal Studios:
classic films come to life with stunning special effect rides.
*** Cypress Gardens:
exotic gardens mixed with spectacular water-ski stunts.
** Church Street Station:
a fabulous entertainment centre that has become an attraction in its own right.
** Wet 'n Wild: the very best way to cool off from the Florida heat.

Opposite: *Lazy River, Wet 'n Wild, is one of Orlando's less hair-raising attractions.*

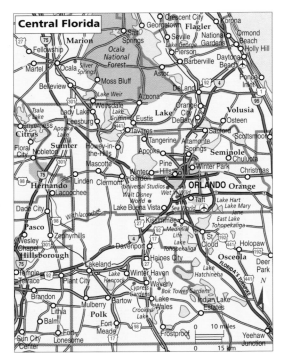

ORLANDO

The city of Orlando, now some 120 years old, was little more than a military outpost until 1875.

It is believed to have been named after **Orlando Reeves**, a soldier who was killed by an Indian arrow while on duty back in 1835. Agriculture dominated the early development, due to a year-round sunny, warm climate and the area's central position in the state. About 40 years ago, corporations began to arrive and the city started to blossom into the thriving metropolis it is today.

The reason that brings most people to this area is Mickey Mouse, and some 13 million tourists who visit the city each year have no other intention than to play in the parks. **Orlando International Airport** receives numerous direct flights from Europe, both scheduled and charter traffic.

It comes almost as a shock to find that Disney does not own the entire territory, so formidable has the image of the little mouse become, but theme parks aside, the downtown area offers an abundance of other interesting diversions. Sports fans, too, are well catered for. **Golfers** will be delighted to find over 130 golf courses within 45 minutes of the city (more than 100 courses within the Greater Orlando area). Course designers include Joe Lee, Tom Fazio and Robert Trent Jones. Others like Nick Price, Payne Stewart, Gary Player and Arnold Palmer all have homes in the city, which hosts at least four major tournaments a year. More than 800 **tennis courts** are available and spectators can choose between **basketball**'s Orlando Magics, American football's Orlando Predators and ice hockey's Oralo Solar Bears.

Charles Hosmer Morse Museum of American Art *

This museum is said to hold the world's largest collection of **Louis Tiffany** stained glass and lamps and also features paintings and furniture, mainly from the late 19th and early 20th century. The entire museum moved to **Winter Park** at 455 Park Avenue in 1996 to more than double its exhibition space. Park Avenue is one of Orlando's top shopping streets, lined with trendy cafés and speciality shops. The whole of Winter Park is known as an upmarket shopping area with glitzy boutiques and art galleries.

Above: *Park Avenue in Winter Park is lined with glitzy boutiques and chic pavement cafés.*

Cornell Fine Arts Museum *

The Cornell Fine Arts Museum on Holt Avenue is part of the **Rollins College** campus and houses the largest collection of European and American art in central Florida.

Harry P Leu Botanical Gardens **

Located at 1730 N Forest Avenue, this is another venue that will delight nature lovers. Established over 100 years ago on a 23-acre (9ha) urban setting, this lavish garden contains the largest **formal rose garden** in Florida. There is also an orchid conservatory, a stunning camellia collection that is in flower from autumn to spring, massive old oak trees and a big floral clock.

Orlando Museum of Art **

This museum at 2416 North Mills Avenue, Loch Haven Park, has a permanent collection of 19-th and 20-th century works, Mayan artefacts and a delightful 'Art Encounter', aimed at children.

CHURCH STREET STATION

This venue comes alive after dark as theme-parked-out visitors take yet another leap into fantasy land. The Church Street Station Historic Train Depot was Orlando's first station and a major stop on the South Florida network. Now Rosie O'Grady's, The Cheyenne Saloon, The Orchid Garden and Phineas Phogg's each pump out themed entertainment while Lili Marlene's, Crackers Seafood Bar and The Cheyenne Barbecue offer some of the best food in town. Kids won't want to miss the home-made ice cream and treats at the Bumby Gift Shop, and the Church Street Station Exchange is a three-storey shoppers' delight of souvenirs and nick-nacks.

THEME PARK BLUES

There is so much to do in Orlando that it is well worth your while planning ahead. Here are a few key pointers:
• Don't cram too much activity into one day.
• If you have young children, hire a pushchair or quit early.
• Be prepared to queue for rides, particularly in the peak summer months.
• Children should wear hats to minimize a risk of sunburn or heatstroke.
• Save time by choosing your priority rides and planning a sensible route between them.
• Don't spend days in a row in the parks; take breaks in between and the kids will enjoy it much more.
• Be warned – every park is a kid's heaven of sweet and gift shops. Don't expect to leave empty-handed.

Below: *Epcot's high-tech wizardry impresses young and old alike.*

WALT DISNEY WORLD

Almost a city in itself, Walt Disney World encompasses the **Magic Kingdom, Epcot** and the **Disney–MGM Studios**, and surrounds Lake Buena Vista to the south-west of the Orlando downtown area. It is easy to spend an entire holiday inside this vast complex with its numerous hotels, over 60 restaurants, shopping malls and at least five golf courses as well as lakes with their own watersports facilities.

The Magic Kingdom ★★★

For many people this park epitomizes Walt Disney World and is the first stop on any visit. Call tel: (407) 824-4321 for opening times. Enchanting **Cinderella Castle** lies at the heart of the Magic Kingdom, its six themed lands radiating outward like the spokes of a wheel. **Main Street USA**, lined with old-time shops and restaurants, leads you from the main entrance to the castle and is the site of the daily **Parade** at 15:00.

Adventureland is home to the quaint **Swiss Family Treehouse**, the sweet tunes of the **Enchanted Tiki Birds**, a steamy **Jungle Cruise** and the rowdy **Pirates of the Caribbean**. The pace picks up a bit in **Frontierland** where you will encounter the first white-knuckle ride – the world's longest flume drop from **Splash Mountain** – as well as the slightly tamer **Big Thunder Mountain Railroad** and **Tom Sawyer Island**. **Liberty Square** takes a look back at America's history. Take a steamboat ride and visit the interesting **Hall of Presidents** and the spooky **Haunted Mansion** filled with cobwebs, apparitions and creepy sounds.

Fantasyland is perfect for little visitors, offering Peter Pan, Dumbo, Mad Hatter's Tea Party and Snow White rides and carousels, and the singing dolls of **It's a Small World**.

Mickey's Toontown Fair is where you'll find Mickey and his friends in a cartoon world brought to life. Stroll along the **Walk of Fame**, where characters' voices are activated by stepping on the stars.

Older visitors will not want to skip **Tomorrowland** and its highlight ride, **Space Mountain**, an unnerving roller coaster in the dark. Nervous visitors may prefer the calmer **Grand Prix Raceway** or the **Alien Encounter**.

Epcot ★★★

Why travel to the ocean when it is brought to you at landlocked Epcot? One of the latest attractions here is the **Dive-Quest** programme of **The Living Seas** exhibit where visitors can spend 40 minutes among the 65 marine species kept in the huge saltwater tanks.

Both educational and fun, the **Future World** section takes visitors from space travel to human health and fitness while **The Land** presents the natural balance to The Living Seas. The 40-acre (16ha) **World Showcase** takes you around 11 different countries of the world and back again from frenetic O Canada! film to the calm of turn-of-the-century Paris.

Disney–MGM Studios ★★

This working film lot offers backstage viewing, and rides inspired by films like *Star Wars*. Indiana Jones comes to life thanks to daredevil stuntmen, and the old-time hit *Sunset Boulevard* plays tribute to legends of the past.

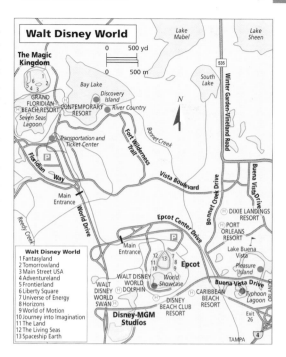

Walt Disney World

The Magic Kingdom

0   500 yd

0   500 m

Walt Disney World
1 Fantasyland
2 Tomorrowland
3 Main Street USA
4 Adventureland
5 Frontierland
6 Liberty Square
7 Universe of Energy
8 Horizons
9 World of Motion
10 Journey into Imagination
11 The Land
12 The Living Seas
13 Spaceship Earth

DISNEY FACTS

• Named after **Walter Elias Disney**, whose dream it was.
• Opened in October 1971.
• Covers a total area of 11,088ha (27,400 acres).
• **Epcot** was opened in October 1982.
• **Disney MGM Studios** opened in 1989.
• Nearby attractions are: Discovery Island, River Country and Typhoon Lagoon.
• Choose from at least seven hotels, villas or apartment complexes inside the park.
• There are over 60 restaurants (22 within the parks).

Right: *Universal Studios offers rides, stunt shows and movie memorabilia.*
Opposite: *Killer whales perform daily at Sea World in Orlando.*

AROUND DISNEY
Mystery Fun House and Starbase Omega *

Fifteen rooms filled with surprises, exciting laser games and an 18-hole miniature golf course. Located at 5676 Major Boulevard. Open 10:00–22:00 daily.

Universal Studios ***

Orlando is not just about the extravagant Walt Disney complex. No visit would be complete without experiencing the fabulous shows, rides and thrills of **Universal Studios**, although this venue appeals mainly to older children and adults. The Studios, located at 1000 Universal Studios Plaza, are open from 09:00 daily.

The recently opened **Terminator 2: Battle Across Time** is billed as the world's first four-dimensional, interactive attraction. But do not miss **Ghostbusters**, **Kongfrontation**, **Earthquake**, **Jaws** or **Back to the Future**, all of which are guaranteed to cause sweaty palms, shrieks and palpitations. Calmer rides include the **ET Adventure** and **Fieval's Playland**. The Studios are on International Drive, not far from Sea World. The company is set to open a second park, the Island of Adventure, in 1998, including a massive Entertainment Zone with a 16-theatre complex which will house a staggering 5000 people. Interactive restaurants and bars, run by sports stars, will all be part of the complex.

GOLFING FACTS

• 123 courses lie within a 45-minute drive of downtown Orlando.
• Nick Price, Lee Janzen, Payne Stewart, Ian Baker-Finch, Gary Player, Corey Pavin and Arnold Palmer are among the golfing stars to own a home here.
• Arnold Palmer, Jack Nicklaus, Tom Fazio and Robert Trent Jones have all designed courses in the area.
• Walt Disney World Resort has six courses alone within the complex.
• The World Cup of Golf was hosted by Lake Nona in 1993 and Grand Cypress in 1991.
• PGA tour events include the Walt Disney World–Oldsmobile Classic and the Bay Hill Invitational. LPGA events include the Chrysler Tournament of Champions and the HealthSouth Classic.

Wet 'n Wild Orlando ★★

This theme park at 6200 International Drive recently added a white-knuckle toboggan ride to its long list of attractions. If you want to get your adrenaline pumping, then don't miss this heart-stopping, six-storey drop down a tunnel. The area includes water slides, flumes, lazy rivers and pools to keep water babies of all ages happy for hours. Open all year round, though times vary according to season.

Ripley's Believe It or Not! Museum ★

A peculiar attraction not to be missed, this rather bizarre museum, also on International Drive, is housed in a strange building made to look as though it is about to collapse and provides odd entertainment for relatively low cost. Open 10:00–23:00 daily.

Sea World ★★

Established in 1973, Sea World, situated on 6227 Sea Harbor Drive, offers the stunning **Wild Arctic**, which combines a flight over the frozen North and close-up encounters with wildlife including polar bears. Other attractions in the park are the **Caribbean Tide Pool**, **Pacific Point Preserve** and **Terrors of the Deep**. Open 09:00–19:00 in winter, 09:00–20:00 in spring and autumn, 09:00–23:00 in summer.

SHOPPING

Shopaholics beware – retail space abounds in Orlando:
- Altamonte Mall, Osceola Mall, Orlando Fashion Square and Seminole Town Center.
- Belz Factory Outlet – over 160 factory discount stores.
- Mercado Mediterranean Shopping Village.
- Park Avenue – upmarket boutiques in Winter Park.
- Theme parks – wide variety of merchandise for sale.
- Airport – for last-minute souvenir hunting.

Nightlife Attractions ★

Evening entertainment is as varied as the theme parks. Venues are highly competitive and forever trying to outdo one another. They also extend the fantasy flavour of Orlando, from **Aloha! Polynesian Luau** at Sea World, where guests are whisked off to Hawaii, to the **Sleuths Mystery Dinner Show** at 7508 Republic Drive, with its six-nightly who-dunnit mysteries ensuring much stimulated dinner conversation. **Capone's Dinner & Show** located at 4740 West Highway 192, Kissimmee, presents a musical about Chicago's prohibition years.

OUT IN THE WILDS

Florida's reserves are divided into state parks and national parks. State authorities look after scenic areas or places of historical importance, while national parks tend to be ecologically important areas needing protection. Many trails, taking anything from one hour to several days, cut through these conservation areas. A mammoth hiking route of 1300 miles (2092km), traversing the entire state, is planned. Check with the local park rangers' office for details of paths. In some areas you need a permit, usually either free or costing US$1 or US$2.

AROUND ORLANDO

Leaving the glittering illusions of Orlando behind, you discover that central Florida has some unspoilt areas that look much the same now as they must have when discovered by the Europeans a few hundred years ago.

To the east, near the town of Christmas, lies the **Tosohatchee State Reserve**, said to be one of the most pristine sites in the region. Visitors are free to roam through the park, along 40 miles (65km) of the **Florida Trail**. During hunting season you are be obliged to wear bright orange warning vests, and it's best to call ahead to warn the park rangers of your arrival. Also to the east of Orlando is an artificial wetland area – the **Orlando Wilderness Park**. This is an excellent place for bird spotting, but is closed during the hunting season which lasts from 1 October to 20 January.

Heading north from Orlando, you pass through **Maitland**. Visit the popular **Art Center**, which promotes American art and artists in an attractive rural setting. Victoriana rules supreme at the **Historic Waterhouse Residence and Carpentry Shop Museums**, which were built in 1884 and maintain their stately Victorian air to this day. Equally interesting are the **Maitland Historical Museum** and the **Telephone Museum**.

Nostalgia is the key note at **Sanford** where the steamboat, *Grand Romance*, puffs along the St Johns River with up to 350 dinner guests on board.

Below: *Glass-bottom boats travel across Silver Springs in search of alligators, fish and turtles.*

Lake County *

Further to the northwest of Orlando, the St Johns River is joined by the Wekiwa River at Apopka, which is the home of the **Wekiwa Springs State Park**. The numerous tributaries feeding into the river form perfect canoeing trails, while energetic hikers can choose from several splendid, well-mapped paths.

Beyond, and pretty as a postcard, the tiny village of **Mount Dora** perches on top of a bluff overlooking Lake Dora. Many of the quaint cottages decorated with flower-filled window boxes are now art galleries and tempting antique shops, reminiscent of New England rather than Florida. **Renninger's Twin Markets**, held here each weekend, attract up to 500 antique dealers.

Lake Dora lies in the heart of Lake County, which was named for its abundance of water. A canal, said to be one of the most beautiful in the world, connects lakes Dora and Eustis and is perfect for relaxing cruises.

Further north, in Marion County, the landscape changes from the typical Florida flatlands to rolling green hills. This lush farmland is filled with cattle and thoroughbred race horses. Some of the 400 horse farms have open days, when visitors can visit the facilities and watch training sessions.

Ocala **

In Ocala be sure to visit the **National Forest** with its sand pine trees and **Silver Springs**, one of the state's oldest attractions and the world's largest natural spring. The Springs contain alligators, turtles and large-mouth bass. Travel on a glass-bottom boat – the water is so clear here that one can see to a depth of 80ft (24m).

Above: *Marion County is home to some of Florida's top horse breeders.*

FISHING

Lake County is named after its 1440 lakes. Many people visit the area in search of peace and quiet after the frenzy of Orlando. Fishing is a popular pastime here, the waters containing some 115 species. The largemouth bass is Florida's official fresh-water fish. If you are over 16 years of age you may need a fishing or hunting licence in some parts of the state. For details of local regulations contact the **Florida Game and Fresh Water Fish Commission**, tel: (904) 488-1960 or 488-2975.

**ANNUAL EVENTS
AROUND ORLANDO**

January • Florida Citrus Festival and Polk County Fair.
February • Silver Spurs Rodeo, held in Kissimmee since 1944.
March • Four-day Kissimmee Bluegrass Music Festival.
April • Polk City week of aviation events.
May • Annual outdoor Art Festival at Lakeland.
June • Bi-annual International Orchid Fair, last held 1996.
October • Florida Horse and Agricultural Festival, Ocala.
November • Chrysanthemum Festival, Cypress Gardens.
December • Florida Citrus Sailfest at Lake Monroe.
Mid-December • Very Merry Christmas Parade, the Magic Kingdom, Walt Disney World.

Or take an exciting jeep safari or jungle cruise. Children will enjoy the **Wild Waters** next to the park, with its giant wave pool, slides and water cannons. For opening times call tel: (904) 236-2121 or 800 274-7458.

The 350-acre (142ha) **Ocala National Forest** incorporates more than 100 miles (160km) of horse trails and 65 miles (105km) of the Florida National Scenic Trail. One of the most enjoyable ways to experience the park is by leisurely canoe or on horseback. There are also dive and snorkel sites.

Among Ocala's attractions is **The Appleton Museum of Art** with its regularly changing exhibitions of antiquities dating back 5000 years. Here you can marvel at early Rembrandt etchings, a 'Thinker' by Rodin (cast from the *original* mould), Turkish prayer rugs, a wooden Tibetan saddle and Japanese figurines. Open 10:00–16:30 Tuesday–Saturday, 13:00–17:00 Sunday.

The distinctly 20th-century **Don Garlits Museum of Drag Racing** houses a collection of antique cars, as well as the famous 'swamp rats' (specialized drag racing vehicles). Open 09:00–17:30 daily, except Christmas Day.

Clermont *

Clermont, to the west of Orlando, is home to the fascinating **House of Presidents Wax Museum**. Figures range from George Washington to Bill Clinton. It is also at the centre of Florida's wine production, and vineyards carpet the landscape. With the help and advice of the nearby University of Florida, the region now produces very palatable wines. **Lakeridge Winery and Vineyards** is open to the public for wine-tasting and tours. The other main crop around Clermont is citrus fruit and from the **Florida Citrus Tower** on Highway 27 you can enjoy a stunning panoramic view across the region.

Kissimmee **

Within easy driving of Orlando, the Kissimmee–
St Cloud area offers plenty of themed entertainment,
some as bizarre as the **Tupperware World Headquarters**,
while managing to retain old world charm. The emphasis
here is on cowboys, rodeos and the outdoors rather than
Mickey Mouse, but the hotels are happy to sell themselves as the perfect spot from which to explore Walt
Disney World, just a few miles north.

Kissimmee is slightly closer to Walt Disney World,
lying on the northwestern tip of **Lake Tohopekaliga**,
while St Cloud lies just a few kilometres to the east on
the southern shores of **East Lake Tohopekaliga**.

As you head south from Orlando along S Orange
Blossom Trail, **Gatorland** is worth a stop to shiver at the
sight of more than 5000 prehistoric-looking alligators and
crocodiles. The park has thrilling daily shows such as
Gator Jumparoo, Gator Wrestling and Snakes Alive, and a
restaurant where gator ribs are on the menu. Open
08:00–dusk. Unless you are a snake phobic, also visit the
Reptile World Serpentarium at St Cloud where visitors
can handle the reptiles and see some of the venom and
antidote production that makes this facility a world
authority on snakes.

Friendlier animals are found at the **Green Meadows
Petting Farm**, which provides a two-hour tour of 300
farm animals, with younger visitors being encouraged to
touch. Open 09:30–16:00 daily; the park closes at 17:30.

HORSE RACING

Ocala gained acclaim as a
centre for horse racing when
a locally bred horse called
Needles was the surprise win-
ner of the **Kentucky Derby**.
Today there are some 400
horse farms in the area, many
of which welcome visitors.
To see the farms and enjoy
the rolling hills and green
countryside, drive south-
west out of Ocala and down
Route 200 towards Holder.
The largest racecourse in
Florida is the **Gulfstream
Park** track between Miami
and Fort Lauderdale where
the US$500,000 **Florida
Derby** is run each March.

Opposite: *Kissimmee is
cowboy country, and
rodeos are held regularly.*
Left: *The safest way to see
alligators is at Gatorland
south of Orlando.*

THE GLADIATORS

For this hit television show, contestants take on athletic Gladiators in a series of games dependent on strength, stamina and reflexes. Since its launch, the American Gladiators contest has led to many similar competitions around the world. Although the show's proper name is **The American Gladiators Orlando Live!**, it is actually filmed in **Kissimmee**. If you'd like to be a spectator, give the local tourist authority a call to find out when the next show is planned.

Splendid China in Kissimmee has miniature recreations of over 60 famous sights in China, including the Great Wall and the Forbidden City. The park also offers live entertainment, a children's playground, shops and Chinese restaurants.

Those with a head for heights and speed can become United States fighter pilots for the day with F-16 trained pilots on hand to teach aerial combat manoeuvres. **Fighter Pilots USA** is based at the town's small airport. Slightly closer to the ground is the **Flying Tigers Warbird Air Museum** on 231 Hoagland Boulevard with its World War II aircraft and flying shows. You can also book a flight for a bird's-eye view of the Orlando area.

Kissimmee–St Cloud has its own water park, **Water Mania**. This 38-acre (15ha) park has all the usual thrills and spills with slides and wave pools as well as Wipe Out, a simulated surf ride.

The **World of Orchids** at 2501 Old Lake Wilson Road houses the first permanent indoor display of orchids in the world, in a conservatory measuring $29,000 \text{ft}^2$ (2700m^2). Recreating the steamy heat of the tropics, the park holds thousands of flowering orchids in a variety of garden settings, hosts three orchid fairs a year and exports its delicate product worldwide.

The attractive Old Town shopping centre contains inviting, old-fashioned shops and restaurants, as well as a giant Ferris wheel and museums.

As in Orlando, most of the evening entertainment venues and restaurants here have climbed on the fantasy bandwagon. **Arabian Nights** (*see* At a Glance p. 61) brings exotic legends to life. **Medieval Life** offers a trip through a spooky dungeon and shows by craftsmen in traditional costumes. **Wild Bill's Wild West Dinner Show** has a local flavour: cowboy antics, native Comanche Indian dancing and square dancing adding a touch of the Ol' West.

Below: *Cypress Gardens, a perfect place to while away a few unforgettable hours.*

Polk County **

Like Lake County further north, Polk County, immediately to the south, is a superb inland retreat, offering nature lovers over 600 **freshwater lakes**. Lining these tranquil lakes are the big, fragrant **citrus groves** and deep, dark **pine forests** that have helped to make the area a major scenic attraction.

This county, however, offers a pleasant mix of natural as well as cultural offerings. The **Black Hills Passion Play**, which depicts the last seven days of Christ's life, is held each spring at the **Lake Wales Amphitheatre**. The big **Polk Museum of Art** is one of the largest museums in central Florida and the **Mulberry Phosphate Museum** houses some interesting displays of petrified dinosaur bones excavated in the surrounding region.

Among the places to visit is **Bok Tower Gardens**. This 128-acre (52ha) expanse provides a sanctuary for both fauna and flora. In the middle of the garden a 57-bell carillon tower chimes the hours, while musicians wander around and a varied programme of year-round concerts is sure to delight music lovers.

By far the more commercialized and better known is nearby **Cypress Gardens**. Over 200 acres (81ha) of lovingly tended park include a stunning variety of over 8000 species of plant from 75 different countries. Also the state's oldest theme park, Cypress Gardens was carved out of the virgin bush by the enterprising Dick and Julie Pope back in 1936. Today it is well known and loved for its spectacular, daring water-ski shows, its performing birds and the southern 'Belles' that stroll around the park in their colourful crinoline dresses. Each year the park tries to develop yet more daring and breathtaking shows in addition to its regular calendar of events.

Above: *Dixieland musicians entertain the crowds at Cypress Gardens.*

LAKE TOHOPEKALIGA

Seminole Indians once lived on the shores of this lake which today separates St Cloud and Kissimmee. The latest attraction here is **Cypress Island**, its 'Wild Encounters' preserve filled with panthers, raccoons and alligators. Explore it on foot, by golf cart or airboat, by day or on night-time photo-safari. The lake is also the setting for special events like the annual Spring Bluegrass Festival, and the autumn Boating Jamboree.

Orlando and Central Florida at a Glance

The **summer** months, from June to October, are **hot** and humid with frequent short **thunderstorms**, but crowds are reduced. The peak **winter** months are **December** to **February**, when Americans abandon the cold northeast in their thousands and head for the winter sun. Parks are packed, but the weather is mild and drier, and so better for queuing.

Orlando International Airport has some 850 flights a day and can handle 5000 passengers an hour. Many European carriers fly direct; United States airlines have good domestic connections. Most hotels offer free **shuttles** from and to the airport. Public **buses** service the downtown area; there are also limo (limousine) and taxi services, both fairly expensive. Orlando and Kissimmee are on Florida's **78 Turnpike Toll Road** from Miami and on **Interstate 4** which crosses the state from Tampa to Daytona Beach. **US192** takes you near the mainentrance of the Magic Kingdom. **Amtrak** offers train services to Winter Park (centre of Orlando), and to Kissimmee.

Driving around Orlando is quite straightforward and International Drive is the main artery. Plenty of **taxis** are available and a number of the attractions offer **shuttle** services from the hotels. **I-Ride** shuttle buses operate a 15-minute service, running from 07:00–24:00. Children ride free of charge.

Orlando
LUXURY
Marriott's Orlando World Center, 8701 World Center Drive, tel: (407) 239-4200, fax: 238-8777. A massive hotel with many facilities, attracting large numbers of convention delegates.

MID-RANGE
Clarion Plaza, 9700 International Drive, tel: (407) 352-9700. Next to the Convention Center, 1.2 miles (2km) from Sea World. **Golden Tulip Las Palmas Hotel**, 6233 International Drive, tel: (407) 351-3900, fax: 352-5597. About 14 miles (20km) from downtown area, but close to the major attractions.

BUDGET
Quality Inn Plaza, International Drive, tel: (407) 345-8585. Over 1000 rooms, conveniently located.

Disney
LUXURY
Grand Floridian, Lake Buena Vista, tel: (407) 934-7639, fax: 354-1866. A grand hotel at a grand price, but very convenient for Disney with a monorail stop outside.

MID-RANGE
Dixie Landings Resort, Lake Buena Vista, tel: (407) 934-7639. Conveniently situated inside Walt Disney World. Southern plantation-house style with a massive swimming pool.

Kissimmee
MID-RANGE
Radisson Inn Maingate, 7501 W Irlo Bronson Memorial Highway, tel: (407) 396-1400, fax: 396-0660. Suitable for families, with children's restaurant, pool and regular shuttles to Disney.

Orlando and Kissimmee have turned dinner theatres into a lucrative art form.

Orlando
Church Street Station, 129 W Church Street, tel: (407) 422-2434. The main dining and entertainment complex downtown. **Hard Rock Café Orlando**, next to Universal Studios, tel: (407) 892-7311. Guitar-shaped building with more than 500 items of rock 'n' roll memorabilia to admire while eating. **Christini's**, 7600 Dr Phillips Blvd, tel: (407) 345-8770. Upmarket northern Italian cuisine, book ahead.

Orlando and Central Florida at a Glance

Disney World
For all Disney restaurant information and reservations, tel: (407) 939-3463.
Magic Kingdom
King Stefan's Banquet Hall. Prime rib, seafood and other meals fit for a king.
Liberty Square
The Liberty Tree Tavern. Recreation of a colonial inn; wholesome American food.
Epcot
The World Showcase. 12 restaurants with menus from around the world.

Kissimmee
Arabian Nights, 6225 W Irlo Bronson Memorial Highway, tel: (407) 239-9223. Dinner show offering Eastern delights such as belly dancing.
Medieval Times Dinner and Tournament, 4510 W Irlo Bronson Memorial Highway, tel: (407) 239-0214. Joust with the knights and toast King Henry during a four-course dinner with unlimited beer, wine and soft drinks.
Wild Bill's Wild West Dinner Show, 5260 W Irlo Bronson Memorial Highway, tel: (407) 351-5151.

SHOPPING
Belz Factory Outlet World, 5401 W Oakridge Rd, Orlando, tel: (407) 352-9600. Over 150 stores offering up to 75% off normal retail prices.
Mercado Mediterranean Shopping Village, 8445

International Drive, Orlando, tel: (407) 345-9393.
Old Town, 5770 W Irlo Bronson Memorial Highway, Kissimmee, tel: (407) 396-48888. Old-world feel with more than 70 speciality shops.
Fleamarkets, Hwy 17-92 between Sanford and Orlando, tel: (407) 647-3976.

TOURS AND EXCURSIONS
Aerial Adventures of Orlando, 3529 Edgewater Drive, Orlando, tel: (407) 841-UPUP. Fly in the Rosie O'Grady Flying Circus balloon.
Central Florida Balloon Tours, PO Box 2764, Winter Park, tel: (407) 294-8085.
St Johns River Cruises, 4359 Peninsula Point, Sanford, tel: (407) 330-1612. Two-hour trip down the river to see alligators, wildlife and birds.
Walt Disney World, **Sea World** and **Universal Studios** offer **guided tours**. Enquire at entrance gates.

USEFUL CONTACTS
Central Florida Convention and Visitors Bureau, 600 N Broadway, Suite 300, Bartow, FL33830-1839,

tel: (941) 534-4370, fax: 533-1247.
Orlando/Orange County Convention and Visitors Bureau, 8445 International Drive, Orlando, FL32819, tel: (407) 363-5892, fax: 363-5899.
Kissimmee/St Cloud Convention and Visitors Bureau, 1925 E Irlo Bronson Memorial Highway, Kissimmee, FL34744, tel: (407) 847-5000, fax: 847-0878.
Lake County Convention & Visitors Bureau, 20763, US Highway 27, Groveland, FL34736, tel: (904) 429-3673, fax: 429-4870.
Walt Disney World Central Reservation Office (for in-park accommodation), Suite 300, Lake Buena Vista, 32830, tel: (407) 934-7639.
Walt Disney World Information, Box 10040, Lake Buena Vista, FL32830, tel: (407) 824-4321.
Golfpac, Box 162366, Altamonte Springs, FL32701, tel: (407) 260-2288. For golfing vacations at over 40 Orlando courses.

ORLANDO	J	F	M	A	M	J	J	A	S	O	N	D
AVERAGE TEMP. °F	49	54	56	63	67	75	75	74	74	67	58	52
AVERAGE TEMP. °C	8	9	13	17	19	23	23	23	23	19	14	11
HOURS OF SUN DAILY	12	12	12	13	13	14	14	14	13	12	12	12
RAINFALL in	2	3	3	2	4	7	8	6	6	3	2	2
RAINFALL mm	53	71	81	55	100	187	197	160	142	71	45	46
DAYS OF RAINFALL	7	8	8	7	9	13	14	12	11	9	7	7

4
The East Coast

Speed is what this part of Florida is known for, from the deafening roar of rockets blasting into space to the burst of action on the Daytona Speedway track. Halfway along lies the **Space Coast**, where the high technology of **Cape Canaveral** and **Titusville's Space Camp**, not to mention the **Astronaut Hall of Fame**, rival for your attention. **Shuttle launches** take place throughout the year and should not be missed. The explosive blast-off of rocket engines contrasts strongly with the tranquillity of the nearby **National Wildlife Refuge** at Merritt Island and the parks surrounding DeLand.

Further north, on the sands of **Daytona Beach**, **Sir Malcolm Campbell** took land speed-records to a new dimension with his earth-shattering drive of 276mph (442kph) back in 1935. Modern speed addicts have to travel out west to the deserts of Nevada to find enough space to beat his times.

The east coast is also about relaxing and enjoying the incredible natural beauty of long sandy beaches, dramatic Atlantic coastlines – and the lure of buried treasure. **Treasure Coast** to the south is named after the spilled contents of countless ships that floundered on the sand bars well within sight of land. Experts claim that some 1800 Spanish galleons were wrecked on these shores more than 400 years ago and that their priceless cargo still remains, awaiting discovery.

Many golf courses and extensive watersports facilities complete the picture of a superb outdoor area with plenty of distraction on offer for the entire family.

DON'T MISS

*** Spaceport USA:** the history of space exploration, rockets and possibly a shuttle launch are the highlights.
** **Daytona Beach:** mecca for car racing enthusiasts.
** **Merritt Island National Wildlife Refuge:** miles of undisturbed sand dunes and excellent bird-watching.
** **Cocoa Beach:** very good surfing and the best spots to watch shuttle launches.
* **Main Street Pier**, **Daytona Beach:** fairground rides and shops on a traditional east coast boardwalk setting.

Opposite: *Rockets dwarf the visitors at Rocket Park, Kennedy Space Center.*

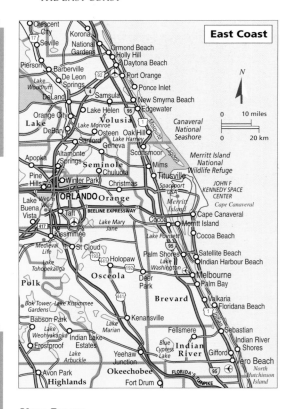

East Coast

VERO BEACH

At the centre of the Indian River citrus belt, the affluent resort of Vero Beach has a healthy mix of industries, but tourism is one of the faster growing. There are some 15 **golf courses** (not all are open to the public), numerous **boat charters** for fishing, canoeing and sailing and several well-maintained **tennis clubs**.

Museums in this city include the **Center for the Arts** on 3001 Riverside Park Drive, which mixes local, national and international exhibitions and is well known for its many seminars, concerts, workshops and festivals. The **McLarty Museum** situated on 13180 N Route, open 10:00–17:00 daily, concentrates mainly on Indian artefacts

Left: *The citrus farming industry made Floridians wealthy at the turn of the century and still provides thousands of jobs.*
Below: *Golf has become big business – Florida has more golf courses than any other American state.*

and recovered treasure and is dedicated to the hurricane of 1715 in which an entire fleet of treasure-laden Spanish galleons perished. The **Mel Fisher Treasure Museum**, at 1322 US1 in neighbouring Sebastian also houses artefacts salvaged from the numerous ships that floundered on this coast. The **Indian River Citrus Museum** takes a look at the industry behind the wealth of the region, while the **Historical Society** has an exhibition at the city railway station; both are located on 14th Avenue. **McKee Botanical Gardens**, on the east side of US1, was first opened in 1932 and its stock of plants is refurbished annually by the Indian River Land Trust.

The **Environmental Learning Center** on Live Oak Drive offers daytime and evening field trips through saltmarsh and mangrove swamp areas, to educate visitors about the surrounding habitat.

The camp site at **Sebastian Inlet State Recreation Area**, to the north of Vero Beach, is flanked by the Atlantic Ocean to the east and the Indian River to the west. Not only good for hiking and cycling, it also has snorkelling and scuba diving opportunities – for certified divers only – and offers some of the best saltwater fishing on the east coast.

BEACHES

Avoid the crowds and head out to the shores of Klondike, Floridana, Canaveral National Seashore and Sebastian Inlet State Recreation Park. Or you can go for fun in the sun with the crowds at Cocoa, Satellite, Indian Harbor and Melbourne Beaches. The best surfing is possible at Cocoa and Playa-linda beaches or Sebastian Inlet.

MELBOURNE

Continue north up Route 1 to find **Melbourne**, a turn-of-the-century city where the emphasis falls on history. The **Brevard Museum of Art and Science**, 1463 Highland Avenue, and the **Brevard Museum of History and Natural Science** in Cocoa both house visiting and permanent exhibitions and displays that tell the story of Florida from the Ice Age to the present. **Brevard Zoo**, 8225 N Wickham Road, has a Paws-On section to amuse children and adults alike and focusses on Latin American animals such as jaguars, llamas and monkeys. Open 10:00–17:00 daily.

At the **Space Coast stadium** you may be able to catch the Florida Marlin baseball team in training. This is also the place where you can enjoy many of the annual festivals which the city stages.

Just inland from Melbourne is **Palm Bay** and the **Turkey Creek Sanctuary**. A prime site for keen bird-watchers, this park is a major calling place for large flocks of **migratory birds**. Spring and autumn residents include rare woodpeckers and martins. **Manatees**, too, may be spotted from the 4000ft (1219m) boardwalk that takes visitors into the centre of the park and past some good bass fishing grounds. Call ahead on tel: (407) 952-3442 to find out when the park is open.

Below: *The Astronaut Memorial Planetarium and Observatory in Cocoa.*

THE SPACE COAST

The Space Coast runs for 72 miles (116km) north–south along Florida's east coast. Although this area is a hub of high-tech activity, it is also a great family destination, a sporting mecca and an eco-friendly environment.

North of Melbourne lies the city of Cocoa, the beginning of the Space Coast. Here you will find the **Astronaut**

Memorial Planetarium and Observatory, where visitors can study images of the surface of Mars, look at the rings of Saturn, or watch comets smashing down on to far-off planets. Call tel: (407) 632-1111 for opening times. Shoppers will enjoy the restored **Old Cocoa Village** area with its brick pavements and cobbled streets.

From Cocoa, cross over **Merritt Island** to reach **Cocoa Beach**, just south of Cape Canaveral. The Atlantic Ocean makes this a surfers' heaven and here you will find the famous (some would say infamous) **Ron Jon Surf Shop** – known by its outrageous billboards that line the coast. A must for shopaholics (even non-surfers will enjoy the spectacle), the shop is open 24 hours a day. A neighbouring park is filled with sand sculptures and includes an 820ft (250m) pier that doubles as a grandstand for shuttle launch viewing; this is a popular spot for fishermen.

Cape Canaveral ★★★

The **NASA Kennedy Space Center** covers 140,000 acres (56,000ha). At its visitor centre, **Spaceport USA**, the public can board tour buses, admire a 6.2 million-pound (2,811,179kg) replica of the shuttle *Explorer* and visit the **Astronaut's Memorial** honouring the memory of the 16 American astronauts who have died in space. Their names are engraved into a polished granite disk which rotates to mirror the sun's movements.

Above: *The Ron Jon Surf Shop in Cocoa Beach has become a mecca for surfers.*

MAN IN SPACE

US President John F Kennedy sparked the space race in 1961. The Russians were ahead since one of their astronauts had already been in space, but Kennedy was determined: Americans would better them and send a man to the moon before the end of the decade. As a result, millions of dollars were pumped into **NASA**, culminating in the launch of **Apollo 11** and the historic moon landing in July 1969. The enormous cost incurred saw the industry going into decline until the launch of the reusable shuttle in 1981. This project, too, was initially fraught with problems. A fatal accident during the take-off of the **Challenger** mission in January 1986 caused a serious setback. The shuttle programme continues, albeit at a slower rate than the scientists would like.

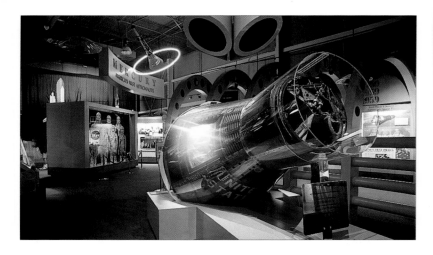

Here you can view **Launch Complex 39** from which the epic **Apollo 11** mission blasted off for the moon on 16 July 1969. Be sure not to miss the outstanding IMAX movies: *The Dream is Alive,* which, astronauts say, feels like the real thing, and *Blue Planet*, a breathtaking look at earth from outer space. Bus trips, split into two different routes – Blue and Red – according to the length of time you wish to spend here, take you on comprehensive **tours** around the complex.

Visitors may inspect further vast launch pads, look at the enlightening astronaut training centres, marvel at bits of meteors and satellites that have fallen from space and take a stroll through the impressive rocket garden. A new state-of-the-art exhibition of America's space transport system features interactive systems of touch screens and audio-animatronics.

Space shuttles still blast off from the complex regularly and a provisional timetable is published every year. Dates may change due to bad weather or for technical reasons, but local tourist authorities are able to advise. Alternatively you can call tel: (+1) 407 867 4636 for recorded information and 800-USA-1969 for general information about the Space Coast.

TURTLE TALK

From May to September, Space Coast beaches come alive as more than 6000 loggerhead, green and leatherback turtles arrive to lay their eggs. The females lumber ashore and laboriously dig nests. Each of the 2000-lb (907kg) animals will lay around 600 eggs (on average, only one nestling will make it to adulthood). After laying their clutches, the nests are covered, and the exhausted giants make their slow way back to the safety of the open sea. Visitors can watch this night-time activity on tours organized by the **Sea Turtle Preservation Society**, tel: (407) 676-1701 between 12:00–15:00.

Titusville ★★

The most northerly city along this stretch of coastline, Titusville boasts a late-19th-century Main Street, now declared a **National Historic District**. It is also a vantage point for **shuttle launches**, and extra parking along the roadside is permitted up to 24 hours before take-off. Modern attractions include the **United States Astronaut Hall of Fame** and the **Valiant Air Command Warbird Museum**, which houses over 350 vintage aircraft, including Flying Tigers and C-47 Transporters, a Sopwith Camel and P-51 Mustang hardships. Flying displays are held annually in March. Open 10:00–18:00 daily, closed on public holidays.

US Space Camp Florida, open 09:00–17:00, allows children to experience the force of gravity and the thrill of aerial acrobatics. The **United States Space Walk of Fame**, filled with an abundance of memorabilia, lies alongside Indian River and overlooks the **Kennedy Space Center** – this is another favoured place for watching NASA shuttle lift-offs.

North Brevard Historical Museum is worth a visit to see the handprints of the original Mercury astronauts, though nature lovers may prefer to explore the **Enchanted Forest**, a lush 400-acre (162ha) hardwood area with cabbage palms, saw palmettos, oaks and vines.

Opposite: *The Astronaut Hall of Fame in Titusville.*
Below: *Children meet a real 'moonwalker' at the Kennedy Space Center.*

Almost opposite Titusville on a spit of land which runs south from New Smyrna Beach to Cape Canaveral is Merritt Island, shared by NASA and the **Merritt Island Wildlife Reserve**. Considered one of the state's leading wildlife viewing areas, it adjoins the Canaveral National Seashore with its 24-mile (39km) beach. There are ranger-led **tours** of the reserve, observation towers for bird-watching and a visitor centre with information about the area. The refuge covers about 220 sq miles ($572km^2$), or 140,000 acres

DAYTONA SPEEDWAY

Races are held from February to the end of October. The first is the **Sunbank 24**, a 24-hour race for sports cars. Trials start in mid-February for the **Daytona 500** stock car race – the classic of the year. By March it is the turn of the bikes, with half a million enthusiasts attending a **Bike Week Festival**. The **Pepsi 400** sees the cars back in July, followed by the **Daytona Pro-Am** in October. The **Bikoberfest** is the year's finale with races and shows.

(56,657ha) and claims to provide a home for more endangered species than any other reserve in the United States. Manatees, bald eagles and loggerhead turtles can all be found here. Both Merritt and Canaveral have boardwalks to take visitors through the dunes and shady hummocks (note that it is against the law to walk on the dunes). Surfing and beachcombing are particularly rewarding along this stretch of coast, though swimming is not recommended due to strong currents and the presence of stinging jellyfish. The best time for bird lovers to visit is winter, when huge flocks of migratory birds mill about.

New Smyrna *

On the way north to Daytona Beach lie the **Sugar Mills Ruins** in Sugar Mill Gardens. Nearby is the small town of New Smyrna, founded in 1770 and was once the largest colony under British rule in the New World. It was developed by a number of enterprising Minorcan, Greek and Italian immigrants, but is today dwarfed by neighbouring Daytona Beach. The scenic **Spruce Creek Canoe Trail** starts and ends at Moody Bridge near New Smyrna Beach; its two loops leading through hardwood forests and salt marsh.

Below: *The New Smyrna Sugar Mill Ruins are a peaceful haven.*

DAYTONA BEACH

Once solely the mecca of car enthusiasts, Daytona Beach has come a long way in its determined effort to become an all-round family destination. The droves of students on spring break, who once numbered some 400,000 annually, have thinned out to a more manageable 250,000 as the city strives hard to clean up its image.

Above: *Cars cruise along Daytona Beach, famous for its stock car and bike races.*

You can still drive your car along the 23 miles (37km) of sands that helped Sir Malcolm Campbell into the record books. But today you need a special permit and may drive at just 10mph (16kph) – it is quicker by bicycle. Up to 500ft (152m) wide in places, the sandy beach is the focus of life in the city. Beach vendors sell everything from hot dogs to T-shirts and you can hire sunbeds, bicycles and sailing boats. Early in the morning surfers head out to catch the first waves of the day, while sailing and jet-skiing competitions are year-round events. Many watersports fans head to the **Halifax River** area where powerboats are available for hire along with deep-sea fishing charters.

Spectators wander along the famous **Boardwalk**, which offers miniature golf, game arcades, fast-food outlets and shops. Equally attractive is the **Main Street Pier**. But those wanting a really good view should take a ride in the overhead gondola.

Shoppers should head to Daytona's two weekly markets. The **Farmers Market** on Bay Street in the downtown area sells fresh fruit and seafood, caught or grown locally. Chefs from many of the town's 400 restaurants do their shopping here. The **Daytona Flea Market** presents 40 acres (17ha) of haggler's paradise. Everything from food to valuable antiques is available here, including some real bargains as well as mountains of tat.

PARTY TIME

February • Grant Seafood Festival, Melbourne: feast on oysters, clams and crabs.
March • Florida Marlins Spring Training, Melbourne: catch a pre-season game. Port Canaveral Seafood Festival, Titusville: fresh fish and gallons of chowder. Valiant Air Command Warbird Air Show, Titusville: a flying spectacular featuring Warplanes of all ages.
Easter Weekend • Easter Surfing Festival, Cocoa Beach.
April • Indian River Festival, Titusville: bikini contests, river raft races and celebrity look-alike competitions. Melbourne Art Festival: almost 300 artists gather to display local arts and crafts.

Right: *The watchtower on the promenade at Daytona Beach.*
Opposite: *Ponce de León Lighthouse towers above its surroundings.*

Situated in the heart of Daytona Beach, the **Halifax Historical Society Museum** on 252 S Beach Street is filled with ancient native American artefacts, Spanish relics unearthed on plantations, more recent war relics, and memorabilia to excite the racing and motoring fraternity – as well as the Gallery of Legends, portraying the development of motor racing and a model of the 1938 Boardwalk. Open 10:00–16:00 Tuesday–Saturday. The **Museum of Arts and Sciences** on 1040 Museum Blvd is worth visiting for its amazing collection of Cuban art brought to the area by former Cuban president Fulgencio Batista, who had a holiday home in the area and bequeathed his collection to the museum. This is also the place to see the impressive skeleton of a prehistoric giant ground sloth measuring 13ft (4m), which was found in the area. The museum is open 09:00–16:00 Tuesday–Friday, noon–17:00 Saturday and Sunday, but closed on public holidays.

The **Peabody Auditorium** presents a succession of concerts throughout the year, frequently featuring famous international names, while the **Daytona Playhouse** puts on plays with the aid of local dramatic talent.

Outside Daytona *

South of town lies the **Ponce De León Inlet Lighthouse**, a wonderful point from which you can view the entire Daytona Beach area. The 100-year-old building remained in use until 1970; since then it has been fully restored as a museum, complete with gift shop.

The Casements in the city of **Ormond Beach**, to the north of Daytona Beach, was once the home of multi-millionaire John D Rockefeller, known locally as Neighbour John. His house has become a cultural centre and museum and is on the National Register of Historic Places. It provides the setting for a whole series of concerts, exhibitions and events, including the **American Indian Festival**, **Annual Christmas Walk** and an interesting **Annual Antique Show**. The house also holds a large and unusual collection of scouting memorabilia. Open 09:00–21:00 Monday–Thursday, 09:00–17:00 Friday, and 09:00–noon Saturday.

Also to the north of the city lies the **Tomoka State Park**. Once the home of Timucua Indians, the area was discovered by Spaniard Alvaro Mexia in 1605. Today it is open for hiking and canoe trails along the Tomoka River; visitors can also book escorted boat tours.

Daytona Speedway **

Henry Ford, **Louis Chevrolet** and **Harvey Firestone** were responsible for establishing Daytona Beach's reputation. They holidayed in the resort at the turn of the century and soon realized that the compact white sands were perfect for car racing.

The **Ormond Hotel** in Ormond Beach was the place to stay in those days and so it was the wide expanse of beach out front that became the racetrack. The first race, held in 1902 between R E Olds and Alexander Winton, resulted in a top speed of 57mph (91kph). By 1935 this had increased to the 276mph (442kph) achieved by **Sir Malcolm Campbell** in his aircraft-engined *Bluebird*.

MARY MCLEOD BETHUNE

Born in 1875 to freed slave parents, Mary McLeod Bethune spent her life campaigning for the black civil rights movement. A friend of Eleanor Roosevelt, she served as a presidential adviser to **Franklin D Roosevelt** and founded the National Council of Negro Women. She also set up Florida's first black girl's school in 1904, with savings of US$1.50 and five pupils. Her white-framed, two-storey house remains filled with awards and mementoes of her life and now forms part of the Bethune–Cookman College campus which has grown up around the original school. Free admission to the public, tel: (904) 255-1401, ext 372, for opening times.

AND MORE PARTYING

July • Space Week
Celebration, Titusville:
achievements in space are
celebrated with a week of
exhibitions and competitions.
September • Labor Day
Pro-Am Surfing Festival,
Cocoa Beach.
October • Seminole Indian
and Florida Pioneer Festival,
Cocoa: indian dancing,
alligator wrestling and local
cooking draw the crowds.
November • Brevard County
Fair, Cocoa Beach: celebration
to mark the start of winter.
Space Coast Art Festival,
Cocoa Beach: over 500
exhibits form the largest
show on the Space Coast.
December • Christmas Boat
Parade, Melbourne: a flotilla
of boats, twinkling Christmas
lights and carolling crews
provide the atmosphere.

Below: *A linesman waves
the chequered flag at
Daytona Speedway.*

The lessons learned by the motor manufacturers down on the beach were later put to good use during World War II, when aircraft designers used the new technology to plan fighter aircraft engines.

Eventually the stock car racers moved south from Ormond Beach, down to a wide patch of sand near Ponce Inlet, attracting thousands of followers. The mass of spectators forced the racers off the sand, and by 1959 the **Daytona International Speedway** on 1801 W International Speedway Boulevard was opened. Stock car racing is still held every summer. The **Daytona 500** takes place in February each year; exciting motorcycle meets are held at the track each March and October; and go-cart racing happens after Christmas.

The latest attraction is the US$18 million **Daytona USA Interactive Motor Sports Center**, open 09:00–17:00 daily. Here you have the chance not only to learn about the history of motor racing, but also to design your very own dream stock car, take part in a pit stop and tour the track.

In addition to its many car and bike races, the Daytona Speedway hosts a series of festivals and fairs to attract owners of vintage cars. A wonderful collection of shiny Corvettes dating back to 1953 forms the proud centrepiece of the **Klassix Auto Museum**.

INLAND PARKS

North of Daytona Beach lies the **Bulow Plantation Ruins State Historic Site** with its 18th-century ruin of a sugar mill destroyed by Seminole Indians. The park has hiking trails, angling spots and a canoe trail through salt marshes, which leads past lovely clusters of magnolia and oak trees.

Above: Tranquil solitude at De León Springs National Park.

Head west down Route 40 to **Barberville**, where the **Pioneer Settlement for the Creative Arts** offers a 45-minute guided tour. The **De León Springs State Recreation Area** nearby, once hailed as a fountain of youth, has trails and good picnic and fishing spots.

South on US15 is **DeLand**, home of the Stetson University and **Gillespie Museum of Minerals** (open 08:00–16:00 Monday–Friday, 09:00–14:00 Saturday). The **DeLand Museum of Art** houses an interesting permanent collection of native American basket work.

DeLand is a short drive from the **Lake Woodruff National Wildlife Refuge** which covers 19,000 acres (7690ha). Canoeists will enjoy the serene waterways, while hikers and cyclists can follow the extensive paths to small pools which attract wildfowl.

South of DeLand is the **Blue Spring State Park**. Manatee sightings here are virtually guaranteed – particularly in winter (November–March), though you can usually find one wallowing in the warm spring water at any time of year. This is also one of the better known inland scuba dive sites, and certified cave divers can explore the waters each spring; snorkelling is also permitted. Camping is available though it is often full, so book ahead.

Just south of the park is the town of **DeBary**, founded by Belgian wine importer Frederick DeBary in the late 19th century. DeBary Hall is the state headquarters for the Florida Federation of the Arts.

RARITIES

The Space Coast is home to over 25 mammal species, 310 types of bird and 700 varieties of fish. Saltwater fish include snapper, flounder, sea trout, grouper, wahoo, sailfish and tuna. Bass, perch (crappie) and bluegill are found in the rivers. The area also contains more federally endangered species than any other area of the United States. Loggerhead, green and leatherback turtles can be spotted, along with Florida manatees, eastern indigo snakes, gopher tortoises, American bald eagles, wood storks, scrub jays and peregrine falcons – all on the endangered list.

The East Coast at a Glance

BEST TIMES TO VISIT

The **summer** months, June to October, are **hot** and **humid** but tempered by cooling sea breezes. Also, the further north you are in Florida, the less chance there is of hurricanes.

Winter is the **peak season** with warm, **balmy days** and less rain, but the crowds are worse, as countless North Americans flood south to escape the icy conditions back home. If there *is* a cold snap (as in January 1996), temperatures in this area will drop to around 40°F (4°C), so pack a coat.

GETTING THERE

Daytona Beach International Airport, 700 Catalina Drive, is served by American, Continental and Delta airlines with a network of domestic services. Melbourne and Vero Beach regional airports serve the Space Coast, but most international travellers will fly direct to Orlando and drive north. Hotels operate **shuttle buses** from the airports and **taxis** are widely available. There are also some shuttle buses from Orlando airport to coastal resorts – check with tourist offices for latest details (*see* Useful Contacts). Daytona and the Space Coast towns are strung along **Highway 1**, which runs inland from the beaches but is the most convenient access route. **Interstate 4** runs from Tampa and Orlando direct to Daytona. All major **car rental** companies are represented in Daytona and along the Space Coast. **Amtrak** operates regular train services down this coast, with stops in Jacksonville to the north and Ocala to the south. **Greyhound buses** make two stops: in Daytona Beach and in Melbourne.

GETTING AROUND

Driving around is very straightforward as all the towns are well signposted. It is a relatively short trip to Orlando and the theme parks (only about 45 minutes from the Space Coast). Travelling south to Fort Lauderdale or Miami is a longer journey of about three hours.

Taxis operate around the clock in towns and they usually have ranks at the major hotels.

Every town has its own **bus service**, and Daytona Beach has a trolley service, **Votran**, running along Atlantic Avenue to take visitors up and down the main strip.

WHERE TO STAY

Accommodation on the Space Coast is very much cheaper than in the Orlando area and prices drop to an average of US$49 per night during the low season, from June to September.

Vero Beach
LUXURY
Disney's Vero Beach Resort, tel: (407) 934-7639. Newly opened hotel bringing Mickey Mouse to the coast.

MID-RANGE
Islander Resort, 3101 Ocean Drive, tel: (407) 231-4431. Has a pool and restaurant but no beachfront.

Melbourne
LUXURY
Radisson Suite Hotel Oceanfront, 3101 N Highway A1A, tel: (407) 773-9260, fax: 777-3190. Spacious suites with beachside balconies, microwave ovens and fridges.

Cocoa Beach
MID-RANGE
Holiday Inn Cocoa Beach Resort, 1300 N Atlantic Ave, tel: (407) 783-2271. On the beach, with a pool and free parking available.
Cocoa Beach Oceanside Inn, 1 Hendry Ave, toll-free: 1 800 874-7958. Rooms have balconies with ocean views; observation deck for shuttle launch viewing.

Daytona
LUXURY
Adam's Mark Daytona Beach, 100 N Atlantic Ave, tel: (904) 254-8200. Beachfront resort; 400 rooms overlooking the ocean, green lawns stretch to the sand.

The East Coast at a Glance

Perry's Ocean-Edge Resort,
2209 S Atlantic Ave,
tel: (904) 255-0581. Popular
luxury beachfront resort with
200 rooms. Good for golfers.

MID-RANGE
Ocean Court Motel,
2315 S Atlantic Drive,
Daytona Beach Shores, tel:
(904) 253-8185, fax: 253-
8187, toll-free: 800 532-7440.
English-owned and operated
oceanfront property.
Maverick Resort, 485 S
Atlantic Avenue, Ormond
Beach, tel: (904) 672-3550,
toll-free: 800 881-2494.
Quiet hotel in residential
area; good off-season rates.

BUDGET
Cardinal Motel,
738 N Atlantic Avenue,
Daytona Beach, tel: (904)
252-1035, fax: 257-3571,
toll-free: 800 555-2819.
Weekly and monthly accom-
modation rates are available.
**Ho-Jo Inn by Howard
Johnson**, 2015 S Atlantic
Avenue, Daytona Beach
Shores, tel: (904) 255-2446,
fax: 673-6260, toll-free:
800 456-2446. Conveniently
situated directly on the beach.

WHERE TO EAT

The central East Coast has a
wide variety of eateries to
suit every budget.
This area prides itself on its
seafood. Annual festivals
celebrate oyster catches,
seafood and river fish.

Vero Beach
Try out the excellent seafood
at either of these:
Ocean Grill, 1050 Sexton
Plaza, tel: (407) 231-5409.
Lobster Shanty,
1 Royal Palm Blvd,
tel: (407) 562-1951.

Cocoa Beach
Rusty's Raw Bar,
2 S Atlantic Avenue.
Enjoy fresh oysters and
bargain seafood buffets.

Daytona Beach
Lighthouse Landing,
4931 Peninsula Dr,
tel: (904) 761-1821.
A good spot to sip cocktails
and watch the sun go
down before enjoying
the fresh seafood.
Cap'n Coty's, 333 Beville
Road, S Daytona, tel: (904)
761-1333. Casual and very
friendly; low-cost seafood
and steak house.

TOURS AND EXCURSIONS

Kennedy Space Center,
tel: (407) 452-2121,
fax: 452-3043. A choice
of informative tours
lasting two hours or longer.

Swampland Tours,
tel: (41) 467-4411. Two-hour
tours to Lake Okeechobee
to spot birds, alligators
and other wildlife.

USEFUL CONTACTS

**Daytona Beach Area
Convention and Visitors
Bureau**, 126 E Orange Ave,
Daytona Beach FL32114,
tel: (904) 255-0415,
fax: 255-5478, toll free:
1 800 854-1234 . Open
09:00–17:00 Monday–Friday.
**Florida's Space Coast Office
of Tourism**, 2725 St Johns
St, Building C, Melbourne
FL 32940, tel: (407)
633-2110, fax: 633-2112,
toll free: 800 USA-1969
for information.
The Tourist Council, Vero
Beach/Indian River County
Chamber of Commerce, 1216
21st St, Vero Beach FL32960,
tel: (407) 567-3491,
fax: 778-3181,
toll-free: 800 338-2678.
**Merritt Island National
Wildlife Refuge**, United
States Fish and Wildlife
Service, PO Box 6504,
Titusville, FL32780,
tel: (407) 861-0667.

DAYTONA BEACH	J	F	M	A	M	J	J	A	S	O	N	D
AVERAGE TEMP. °F	58	59	64	69	75	79	81	81	79	73	66	60
AVERAGE TEMP. °C	14	15	18	21	24	26	27	27	26	23	19	16
HOURS OF SUN DAILY	12	12	12	13	13	14	14	14	13	12	12	12
RAINFALL in	3	3	3	2	3	6	5	6	6	4	3	3
RAINFALL mm	76	76	76	51	76	152	127	152	152	102	76	76
DAYS OF RAINFALL	7	8	8	7	9	13	14	12	11	9	7	7

5
The Northeast

An area of immense contrast, the beautiful Northeast region contains both the oldest and youngest of Florida. This was where the Spaniards first gained a strong foothold in the state, and also where the first sky-scraper was completed in 1901.

Jacksonville is the capital of the region and covers the largest area of any city in the United States. Divided by the **St Johns River**, the city is a mix of modern skyscrapers and historical sites. It is also home to the country's largest brewery and gourmands will enjoy the riverside restaurants and cafés that give Jacksonville such a rich cosmopolitan flavour.

To the north lies **Fernandina Beach**, one of the nation's oldest cities, while to the south lies **St Augustine** where the oldest schoolhouse vies for attention with the oldest shop, the oldest church and the oldest fort.

The Northeast has miles of sensational beaches and picturesque lakes and rivers. Its proximity to Georgia and the rest of the United States helped the area develop as a tourist destination back in the last century. Today, although many visitors drive on south, there is still plenty to stop for.

Wildlife abounds in the deep forests and wide lakes, and **St Augustine Alligator Farm** is one of the most popular attractions. The proud history of the area is brought to life with a series of colourful festivals and realistic re-enactments throughout the year, while the younger cities contain a wealth of cultural activity and a wide range of shopping opportunities.

Don't Miss

*** The Spanish Quarter, St Augustine: restored to its former 17th-century glory.
** The Riverwalk, Jacksonville: shops and bars, many restaurants and street entertainment.
** St Augustine Alligator Farm: birds, monkeys and tortoises, as well as alligators.
** Amelia Island beaches: some of the very best in the Northeast, with high dunes.
** Marjorie Kinnan Rawlings' house: Cross Creek home of the Pulitzer prize-winning novelist.

Opposite: *The 'Stars and Stripes' flies out in St Augustine.*

ST AUGUSTINE

With more than 60 different historic sites and attractions, St Augustine has plenty to offer. The city claims to be North America's oldest town although this title is hotly disputed by Pensacola in northwest Florida. What is clear is that St Augustine is the oldest continuously inhabited town in the United States. It was first settled in 1565 by the Spanish and several of their original buildings can still be visited today. A host of annual festivals helps to retain its historical appeal and brings the old world back to life. To explore the historic zone in the centre of town, either take a horse-drawn carriage tour or, better still, venture forth on foot. A good place to start is at the old **City Gate** (top of **St George Street**). Not only is this close to the main visitor information centre, but it also adjoins the **Castillo de San Marcos National Monument**, built by the Spanish in 1672. The unique material they used was *coquina*, a soft limestone made from broken shells and coral. The fort is surrounded by a moat and comes complete with turrets and walls 16ft (5m) thick. Visit the garrison rooms and try to catch one of the artillery demonstrations that are held on the gun deck.

At Number 14 St George Street you will find the quaint **Oldest Wooden Schoolhouse**, built before the American Revolution out of cypress and red cedar wood. A little further down the road is the **Spanish Quarter**, a fully restored and functional historical village with craftspeople making candles, weaving or spinning. All the items made here are used to continue the upkeep of the Quarter.

St Augustine (map)

Castillo Dr.
San Marcos Ave
Castillo de San Marcos National Monument
City Gate
Orange Museum Theater
Oldest Wooden Schoolhouse
St George
Sevilla
Spanish
Cuna
Cordova
Hypolita
San Sebastian
Ponce de Leon Blvd
Saragossa
Charlotte
Avenida Menendez
Spanish Quarter Museum
Carrera
Riberia
Treasury
Valencia
Basilica Cathedral of St Augustine
Sevilla
Lightner Museum
Cathedral Pl.
Plaza de la Constitution
Bridge of Lions
Alligator Farm
Malaga
King
Zorayda Castle
Potter's Wax Museum
Artillery
Cadiz
Oldest Store Museum
Bravo
La Quinta
Riberia
Cedar
Granada
Ribera
Avenida Menendez
Bravo
De Soto
Bridge
Bridge
Cordova
Washington
St George
Charlotte
Marine
Matanzas
N
Anastasia Island

0   250 m
0   250 yd

At the point where St George Street and Cathedral Place meet, stands the lovely **Basilica Cathedral of St Augustine.** This has undergone various renovations and remodelling, particularly after a fire in 1887. But it still houses parish records dating back to 1594, the oldest known written records in the United States.

Above: *The Oldest Wooden Schoolhouse dates back to British colonial times.*
Opposite: *Inside the quaint Oldest Store Museum.*

The **Plaza de la Constitution** was the centre of the original settlement and today houses a monument to the Spanish constitution of 1812 and a statue of Juan Ponce de León, the first European to set foot in Florida, back in 1513. The **National Archaeological Park** on Magnolia Avenue commemorates his quest to find the Fountain of Eternal Youth (*see* p. 10).

Turn left off St George Street on to King Street and then right into Artillery Lane to find the **Oldest Store Museum**, displaying some 100,000 items that would have been sold at the turn of the century, such as lace-up corsets, medicine containing 90% alcohol(!) and red flannel underwear. The shop attendants all wear authentic costumes. A little further down the lane is the **Oldest House**, which, under the auspices of the local historical society, has been preserved to reflect the life of its various owners; each room's decor illustrating a different era of its occupation.

Back on King Street you'll find **Zorayda Castle**, a reproduction of Spain's Alhambra, with treasures from around the world. The **Lightner Museum**, a few doors along, occupies the former Hotel Alcazar and exhibits 19th-century collectibles. Antique music boxes are a speciality and the attendants happily give demos.

The **Mission of Nombre de Dios**, on San Marco Avenue, is believed to have been the site where America's first mass was celebrated.

ST AUGUSTINE ALTERNATIVES

Potter's Wax Museum, 17 King Street: contains 170 historical figures, a wax workshop and shop.
Ripley's Believe It or Not! at 19 San Marco Avenue: unusual museum filled with oddities from around the world, an amusing place to while away an hour or two.
St Augustine Alligator Farm, 999 Anastasia Blvd: be sure to catch the alligator show when a keeper gets terrifyingly close to the jaws of the animals; the only place to house all 22 species of the world's crocodiles and alligators. Call ahead for show times on tel: (904) 824-3337. Open daily 09:00–17:00.

Above: *The modern sky-scrapers of Jacksonville overlook the St Johns River.*
Opposite: *Jacksonville is home to a large brewing industry.*

THE BEACHES

St Augustine: the start of more than 20 miles (30km) of beach running northwards. Extremely popular, particularly at weekends.
Ponte Vedra: million-dollar homes and golf courses line this stunning beach, the most southerly of the Jacksonville Beaches. Public access to the sand is limited but worth the hunt for crowd-free sunning and shell collecting.
Jacksonville: a mix of commuters who travel into the city and tourists wanting to enjoy the beach.
Neptune: very much quieter, mostly a residential area.
Atlantic: lively area hemmed by restaurants, bars and disco. Great surfing.

JACKSONVILLE

Named after General Andrew Jackson back in 1822, this city began as a tiny town called Cowford nestling on the banks of the St Johns River. Today it spreads out over the largest area of any city in the United States, is one of the most vibrant and, although bypassed frequently on tours of the state, has plenty to offer. Some of the downtown area can be explored by water taxi and by a futuristic monorail, but you need a car to reach the other attractions. It's worth planning trips carefully to avoid spending the day criss-crossing the river.

The **north side** of the downtown area is home to the city's Convention Center and **River City Playhouse**, staging both adults' and children's theatre, as well as the Courthouse, City Hall and Chamber of Commerce.

The **Florida Theatre** on E Forsyth Street is considered the cultural heart of the city and stages more than 100 events annually. The **Cummer Gallery**, on the northwest bank of the river on Riverside Avenue, houses a fine art gallery, displays of early Meissen porcelain and an art education centre. Open 10:00–17:00 Tuesday–Friday, noon–17:00 Saturday and 14:00–17:00 Sunday.

On Zoo Road and bordering the Trout River is **Jacksonville Zoo** (open 09:00–17:00 daily, except public holidays). It houses 700 animal species, many in enclosures that imitate their natural habitat as in the African veld section. You can reach the zoo by water taxi. Only a short distance away is the **Anheuser–Busch Brewery** on Busch Drive, where visitors can join a conducted tour of the plant to learn more about the beer-making process. Afterwards enjoy a brew in the sampling room of the largest brewery in the United States. Open 09:00–16:00, Monday–Saturday.

Jacksonville Landing *

The Landing on Independence Drive is a collection of shops and restaurants, many of which overlook the river, and has entertainers performing in the fountain plaza. It can be reached by water taxi.

The **Riverwalk** on the south bank extends for some 1.2 miles (2km), has a fountain that is lit at night, a marina, water taxi station, restaurants, shops and street vendors. It leads to the **Jacksonville Museum of Science and History**, which incorporates an interactive Children's Museum. Call tel: (904) 396-7062 for opening times.

The **Alexander Brest Museum**, on the campus of Jacksonville University, houses exhibits of Steuben glass, Boehm porcelain and pre-Columbian artefacts. The **Jacksonville Art Museum** on Center Drive has oriental porcelain and artefacts dating from 3000BC to AD1500.

Fort Caroline National Memorial on 12713 Fort Caroline Road contains a model of the original fort. Open daily 09:00–17:00, closed Christmas.

AMELIA ISLAND

The only part of the United States to have flown eight different flags, this 13-mile (21km) island has escaped much of the commercialism apparent elsewhere in Florida. The charming main town, Fernandina, was once the hotbed of pirates.

The **Museum of History** and **St Peter's Episcopal Church**, which served as a school for freed slaves, are worth a visit. Three miles (5km) north is the **Fort Clinch State Park** with a brick fort built by Americans to protect Georgia from further British intrusion after the 1812 war. The fort was only used during the 1847 Civil War when it was occupied by the Confederacy.

DATES TO REMEMBER

1562 French Huguenots establish a colony at Fort Caroline on St John's River.
1565 Pedro Menéndez de Avilés founds St Augustine.
1727 Oldest surviving house in St Augustine is built.
1822 Town of Cowford is renamed Jacksonville after General Andrew Jackson.
1832 William J Mills becomes first mayor of Jacksonville.
1864 Florida's only major Civil War fight, the Battle of Olustee, takes place.
1901 A huge fire destroys downtown Jacksonville.
1908 Jacksonville starts to gain a reputation as the winter film capital with the opening of a major studio.

Below: *The entrance of the recently opened Harn Museum in Gainesville.*

GAINESVILLE

Tourism officials around Gainesville call the area 'The Original Florida' because of its small towns filled with history, its bubbling springs and tiny fishing villages. Gainesville, the centre of the region, is the cultural capital of the area, home of the **University of Florida**. The campus houses the **Florida Museum of Natural History**, which contains fascinating displays taking you from dinosaurs to virtual reality. Open 10:00–17:00 Tuesday–Saturday, 13:00–17:00 Sunday.

The **Harn Museum** on Hull Road is one of Florida's latest institutions, exhibiting African, American and pre-Columbian artefacts across 62,000ft² (19,000m²) of gallery space. The **Fred Bear Museum** on Archer Road is dedicated to the art of archery and contains artefacts dating back to the Stone Age. Open 10:00–18:00 Wednesday–Sunday.

Be sure to visit beautiful **Kanapaha Botanical Gardens** on 63rd Boulevard. This is the second-largest garden in Florida and claims to be the most diverse.

In the downtown area indoor cultural activities take place at the **Center for the Performing Arts** which opened in 1992. Elsewhere, Constans Theater offers student productions that have been sponsored by the Florida Theater Department, while the Gainesville Community Theater puts on shows with other promising local talent. The Hippodrome State Theater by contrast, presents plays with international and national stars and is surrounded by pavement cafés, studios, bars and clubs.

South of Gainesville, down US441, the **Paynes Prairie State Preserve** is extremely popular with campers, hikers, horse-riders and canoeists. This area was once home to native Americans and artefacts found here date back to 7000BC. Some wild cattle, horses and alligators are among the permanent residents.

Left: *Famous novels such as* The Yearling *were written on this typewriter, which can still be seen at the Marjorie Kinnan Rawlings State Historic Site.*

A few miles away on Interstate 75 lies the Timucuan Indian village of **Micanopy**. The Spanish also made their home here, but little is left of anything predating 1821. Today the spot, which is filled with antique shops, is popular with film producers as an old world setting. Every autumn the village hosts a major antique market, attracting up to 200 dealers.

To the southeast is the **Marjorie Kinnan Rawlings State Historic Site**. The Pulitzer award-winning author of *The Yearling* made her home here in the 1920s and faithfully recorded the life she experienced around her in another novel, *Cross Creek*. Her typewriter still stands on the rather rickety porch, her letters and cuttings are on display, and a cupboard door stands ajar to reveal the place in which she hid her bottle of whisky during the Prohibition years.

Be warned: only 10 people can enter the house at a time and there is often a queue, so bring a picnic for the wait, tour the gardens and visit the author's grave a few miles off at Island Grove. Open 10:00–16:00 daily. Note that tours are not available August–September.

Travel north from Gainesville for 2 miles (3km) up the Millhopper Road to reach the **Devil's Millhopper State Geological Site**, a huge swallow-hole just over 120ft (35m) deep. At this marvellously picturesque site, streams tumble over the edge of a chasm amid surroundings of lush, exotic ferns and trees.

CIVIL WAR BATTLE

Both sides claimed victory after Florida's only Civil War battle which took place in the pine forests around Olustee, 13 miles (21km) east of Lake City and some 19 miles (30km) north of Gainesville. In February 1864 about 5000 Union troops moving east from Jacksonville confronted the same number of 'Rebels' for a five-hour battle that left some 300 dead and about 2000 wounded. The site is marked with a memorial and visitor centre. Once a year the forests come alive with soldiers as the battle is re-enacted.

The Northeast at a Glance

The **Northeast** is much **cooler** than the Florida Keys, though temperatures rise dramatically in summer. Most **rain** falls in **summer**, but sea breezes keep the humidity down along the coast. From October to the end of March, temperatures drop and warmer clothes are needed.

Jacksonville International Airport, tel: (904) 741-2000, lies 10 miles (16km) north of the city and is accessible by bus or taxi. Road connections are good – **Highway 1** leads all the way down the east coast, from Jacksonville to Miami. **Interstate 95** comes through Jacksonville, and bypasses St Augustine before heading further south. To drive inland from Jacksonville, use **US90** which leads west to Tallahassee, crossing **Interstate 75** which heads south to Gainesville and Tampa. Rail connections in this part of Florida are poor. **Greyhound bus** services are good with north–south links and cross-country trips from Jacksonville, St Augustine and Gainesville.

Jacksonville's **water taxi** service sails up and down the St Johns River linking most of the major attractions on either shore and operating at 15-minute intervals.

Land-based taxis are easy to hire, though in Jacksonville water taxis are often much more useful. The local **bus** system is geared mainly for residents not tourists, and does not operate its full network late in the evening. All major **car rental** agencies have desks at the airport and in downtown Jacksonville. **St Augustine** is one of the few cities where tourists really ought to **walk** to take in the sights. The historic centre is compact and easy to navigate. If you have little time to spare, take a **trolley ride** or horse-drawn carriage tour. Boat and train tours are also available.

St Augustine
LUXURY
Ponce de León Golf and Conference Resort, 4000 US Highway 1 N, tel: (904) 824-2821, fax: 824-8254. Plenty of space and old-world charm, making a pleasant escape from the narrow streets of the historic town.

MID-RANGE
Days Inn Beach, 2475 A1A, tel: (904) 461-9990. On St Augustine Beach; has a pool, and jacuzzis in the suites.

BUDGET
Casa Blanca Inn, 24 Avenida Menendez, 32084, tel: (904) 829-0928. Waterfront bed and breakfast establishment.

Ponte Vedra
LUXURY
Marriott at Sawgrass, 1000 TPC Blvd, tel: (904) 285-7777, fax: 285-0259. Luxury golf and tennis resort.

Jacksonville
LUXURY
Omni Jacksonville Hotel, 245 Water St, tel: (904) 355-6664, fax: 350-0359. Large rooms, lots of glitz.

MID-RANGE
Doubletree Club Hotel Jacksonville, 4300 Salisbury Road, tel: (904) 281-9700, fax: 281-1957. Right in the heart of the business district.

BUDGET
La Quinta Inn, 8255 Dix Ellis Trl, 32256-8209, tel: (904) 731-9940, fax: 731-3854.

Amelia Island
LUXURY
Amelia Island Plantation, 3000 First Coast Highway, tel: (904) 261-6161, fax: 277-5159. Offers a golf course and hiking trails through 1300 acres (526ha) of grounds.

MID-RANGE
Elizabeth Pointe Lodge, 98 S Fletcher, tel: (904) 277-4851. Bed and breakfast establishment situated on the beach.

The Northeast at a Glance

BUDGET
Hoyt House, 804 Atlantic Avenue, 32034, tel: (904) 277-4300. Bed and breakfast with only nine rooms.

Gainesville
MID-RANGE
Radisson Hotel Gainesville, 2900 SW 13th St, tel: (904) 377-4000, fax: 371-1159. Overlooking the Bivens Arms Lake and close to the University of Florida campus.

BUDGET
Scottish Inn North, 4155 NW 13th St, 32609, tel: (904) 376-2631. Near the airport.

WHERE TO EAT

St Augustine
Oscars Old Florida Grill, 614 Euclid Avenue, tel: 829-3794. Cheap and cheerful, with bluegrass music. Seafood, steaks and burgers are served.

Jacksonville
The Silver Spoon, Jacksonville Landing, tel: (904) 353-4503. Cheerful, offering simple food.
Ciao Gianni, Jacksonville Landing, tel: (904) 353-2626. Fine Italian food.
L&N Seafood, Jacksonville Landing, tel: (904) 358-7732. Well-known seafood restaurant.
Shogun, 10055 Atlantic Blvd, tel: (904) 724-8883. Lots of razzmatazz and delicious Japanese food.

Amelia Island
The Palace Saloon, Center Street, tel: (904) 261-9068. A colourful and atmospheric watering hole with links to Amelia Island's pirate past.
Posada San Carlos, tel: (904) 261-7378. Best known for its movie role as Pippi Longstocking's house.

TOURS AND EXCURSIONS
St Augustine Scenic Cruise, St Augustine Municipal Marina, tel: (904) 824-1806. Interesting 75-minute cruises along the city waterfront and Matanzas Bay. Evening trips are available from 1 April to 15 October.
St Augustine Sightseeing Trains, 170 San Marco Ave, tel: (904) 829-6545. A 7-mile (12km) tour past no less than 80 points of interest. Passengers may get off at any of the 19 stops.
Anheuser–Busch Brewery, 111 Busch Drive, Jacksonville, tel: (904) 751-8116. Informative tours of the brewery and at the end, a welcome stop in the hospitality room to sample the cold beer.

Riverwalk Cruise Lines, tel: (904) 398-0797, and **Annabel Lee**, tel: (904) 396-2333, both offer dinner cruises along the St Johns River, as well as day trips from Jacksonville.

USEFUL CONTACTS
St Augustine–St Johns County Chamber of Commerce, 1 Riberia St, FL32084, tel: (904) 829-5681, fax: 829-6477.
Jacksonville and the Beaches Convention and Visitors Bureau, 3 Independent Drive, FL32202, tel: (904) 798-9148, fax: 798-9103.
Amelia Island Tourist Development Council, 102 Center St, Fernandina Beach, FL32035, tel: (904) 277-0717, fax: 261-6997.
St Augustine Visitor Information Center, 10 Castillo Dr, St Augustine, tel: (904) 824-3334.
Alachua County Visitors and Convention Bureau, 30 E University Ave, Gainesville, FL 32601, tel: (904) 374-5231, fax: 338-3213.

JACKSONVILLE	J	F	M	A	M	J	J	A	S	O	N	D
AVERAGE TEMP. °F	53	55	61	68	74	79	81	81	78	69	61	55
AVERAGE TEMP. °C	12	13	16	20	23	27	27	27	26	22	16	13
HOURS OF SUN DAILY	12	13	13	13	13	14	14	14	13	12	12	12
RAINFALL in	3	3.5	3.5	3.5	5	5	6.5	7	7	3	2	2.5
RAINFALL mm	76	89	89	89	127	127	142	179	179	76	51	63
DAYS OF RAINFALL	8	9	9	9	11	11	12	13	13	8	7	8

6
The Northwest

The Northwest, or **Panhandle** as it is often called, is bordered by Alabama to the north and Georgia to the northeast. This area is also known as the **Emerald Coast** after the vivid greens and rich blues of the sea that contrast starkly with its white beaches.

The Northwest has had a totally different development pattern from the rest of the state. The first area to be won over by the Americans, it was also the most closely involved in the Civil War. Industry and agriculture have been linked to northern neighbouring states rather than the citrus belt to the south.

Early settlers tried their luck in **Pensacola**, but a combination of disease and hurricanes forced them out and it was St Augustine that became the first established colony in Florida. The two cities have since argued fiercely over which is the oldest settlement in the United States, which led to **Tallahassee** becoming state capital as a compromise. Tallahassee is closer to Atlanta than to Miami, and magnolias and live oaks rather than palm trees colour the scenery.

Beyond the historic towns, the region is studded with springs, forest reserves, tunnels, caves and coastal parks, including the **Florida Caverns State Park** with its intriguing calcite formations. Other interesting parks include the **Natural Bridge Battlefield State Historic Site**, where Confederate soldiers once battled to save Tallahassee from falling into enemy hands, and the **Torreya State Park** with its 150ft (46m) bluffs towering high above the Apalachicola River.

Opposite: *One of the many spectacular sunsets on the northwestern Panhandle.*

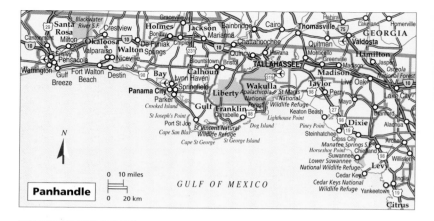

Panhandle

GULF OF MEXICO

PENSACOLA

First inhabited in 1559 by a group of Spanish settlers headed by Don Tristan De Luna, Pensacola is extremely proud of its history and the fact that it has been ruled by five nations. The Spanish, after abandoning their original settlement, returned in 1698 to build a fort at the site of the present day Naval Air Station. Subsequently, control of the city shifted uneasily between the Spanish and British, until it became part of the United States in 1821 with General Andrew Jackson as its first governor.

The **Civil War** divided the city, with Southerners holding Fort McRee and the Yankees holed up in Fort Pickens on the offshore island of Santa Rosa (today's

Pensacola Beach, which is the site of most of the resort hotels). The 'rebels' finally fled and Pensacola was taken for the North. In 1886, little **Fort Pickens** became the city's first real tourist destination as eager crowds flocked to catch a glimpse of the prominent and feared Apache chief, **Geronimo**.

Seville, Palafox and North Hill **

Starting at the west end of **Three Mile Bridge** you first reach the historic district of **Seville**. Once the centre of the Spanish town, it is now a mix of Creole and Victorian homes dating from the 1780s, many of which have been restored, and converted into shops or restaurants. The centre of this area, **Seville Square**, is surrounded by live oaks and provides the setting for the annual Greater Gulfcoast Arts Festival, held on the first weekend of November, which attracts in excess of 100,000 people, as well as the Jazz- or Springfest, a three-day event in April. Off to one side is Alcaniz Street with St Michael's Cemetery containing several thousand graves, some over 200 years old.

To the west lies **Palafox Historic District**. Wrought iron balconies grace Spanish architecture in what was once the commercial district of old Pensacola. Walking on, you reach **North Hill Preservation District**, an upper-class neighbourhood from the 1870s with examples of Queen Anne, neoclassical, Mediterranean and Tudor Revival architecture. It was built on the site of an old fortress, and people still find cannonballs in their gardens.

South of North Hill lies **Historic Pensacola Village** (open 10:00–16:00 Monday–Saturday), commemorating the city's past 200 years in a series of exhibitions. The **Museum of Industry** concentrates on the economic past, while old **Christ Church** houses the Pensacola Historical Museum. Other sites include the Julee Cottage Museum of Black History, Lavalle House and Quina House.

The **Pensacola Museum of Art** on Jefferson Street once served as a prison. Further down the street, the old city hall has become the **TT Wentworth Jr Florida State Museum** and now houses a very interesting Kidstown display on the second floor, guaranteed to delight children of all ages.

> **THE SKY'S THE LIMIT**
>
> The **National Museum of Naval Aviation in Pensacola** has one of the largest collections of military aircraft. Don't miss the west wing with four blue Angel Skyhawks in diamond formation. **Veteran's Memorial Park** is the first replica of the Vietnam Veteran's Memorial in Washington DC. **Eglin Air Force Base** at Fort Walton Beach has the world's biggest environmental test chamber and a windshield preview of the 33rd Tactical Fighter Wing, known as the 'Top Guns' of the Gulf War. **The United States Air Force Armament Museum** nearby is protected by B-17s, SR-71 Blackbird spy planes and aircraft from four wars.

Opposite: *Many of Pensacola's houses date back to the 1780s.* **Below:** *The National Museum of Naval Aviation in Pensacola.*

PERDIDO KEY

Protecting Pensacola to
the south, Perdido Key has
become a popular tourist
destination in its own right,
with bridge connections to
both Florida and Alabama.
Most tourist development is
in high-rise condominiums
and hotels overlooking the
Gulf or the Old River.
Part of the Gulf Islands
National Seashore, the island
contains the **Perdido Key
State Recreation Area** and
Big Lagoon State Park
with a 40ft (12m) lookout
tower for bird-spotting
over the marshes.

DESTIN/FORT WALTON

Spread along 24 miles (38km)
of sugar-white sand coast
with brilliant green waters,
the Destin/Fort Walton beach
towns deserve the **Emerald
Coast** accolade.
With the 100-fathom curve
closer to shore in this
area than anywhere else,
Destin–Fort Walton has the
speediest deep-water access
in the Gulf and some of the
best shells around. Fishing and
seafood are excellent, sailing
and watersports abound.
The area is also renowned for
golf, with 545 holes designed
around woods and wetlands.

PANAMA CITY

Citizens of Panama City are incredibly proud of their mag-
nificently white soft beach, and with good reason. In 1994
the stretch of beach at St Andrews State Park was declared
the best in America by the University of Maryland's labora-
tory for coastal research. The young crowd agrees, and
each spring some 500,000 American students descend for
their traditional spring break. Made legendary by
Hollywood, spring breaks are known for riotous behaviour and some Florida cities have been eager to persuade
the students to move on. Panama City, however, extends a
warm welcome while encouraging consideration for other
visitors. Panama City Beach is also a favourite with families because of its lower costs, excellent facilities and more
than 300 days of sunshine per annum, as well as a growing
reputation for tasty seafood dishes.

Local Attractions ★★

The city is divided by St Andrews Bay with Panama City
lying to the east and Panama City Beach 5 miles (8km)
west. Most visitor attractions are on the beach. The
Museum of Man in the Sea on 17314 Back Beach Road
presents a history of diving and the underwater world.
Gulf World on 15412 Front Beach Road has four shows
daily featuring dolphins, penguins and sea lions. There is
also a tropical garden, scuba diving and shark feeding
demonstrations. Call tel: (904) 234-5271 for opening times.

Left: *Interesting exhibits at the Museum of Man in the Sea, Panama City.*
Opposite: *Fort Walton Beach, one of many stunning white beaches along the Emerald Coast.*
Below: *The Emerald Coast is great sailing territory.*

For some fun in the sun why not try the 6-acre (2½ha) **Shipwreck Island Water Park** slightly further east, which encompasses adrenaline-pumping, white-knuckle rides as well as leisurely, gentle glides down the Lazy River. The **Miracle Strip Amusement Park** next door offers another 30 different rides, including a 2000ft (600m) roller coaster and other thrilling entertainment. The park is closed in winter.

Zoo World lies on the eastern tip of Front Beach Road. Approximately 300 different animals are kept here in simulated natural habitats. There is a petting section (a favourite with many of the younger visitors), a giraffe feeding platform and a splendid walk-through aviary.

Another attraction is the **Bay County's Junior Museum** on 1731 Jenks Avenue, where children can play Indian games and explore a tepee, a log cabin and a pioneer village, as well as a nature trail. Open 13:00–16:30 Tuesday–Friday, 10:00–16:00 Saturday, 13:00–16:00 Sunday.

The **Visual Art Center of Northwest Florida** is on E Fourth Street. Exhibits change every six weeks and visitors are encouraged to join classes or workshops.

The award-winning **St Andrews State Area** at the southeastern tip of Panama City Beach, covers 1260 acres (510ha). It has two fishing piers, watersports facilities and picnic sites, and its beaches are a paradise for beachcombers; there are also camping facilities.

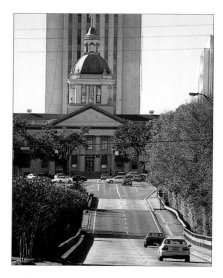

Above: *The new towers above the Old Capitol building in Tallahassee.*
Opposite: *The fine façade of the Supreme Court.*

TALLAHASSEE

Billed as 'Florida with a Southern accent', Tallahassee is a town of historic homes set amid plantations and magnolia trees, bustling with politics and commerce. It also makes a good base for exploring nearby scenic attractions and soaking up the plentiful history and culture of the area.

City Hall, the Old and the New Capitol *

The **Old Capitol** is situated on the corner of the Apalachee Parkway and S Monroe Street and was opened in 1845 when the city was declared the state capital. Altered in 1902, the stately building has retained its magnificent stained-glass dome, as well as the impressive rotunda and political chambers. It takes about 45 minutes to view all the exhibits inside, outlining Florida's history and political evolution.

The **New Capitol** comes alive during the political session (March–May). The 22nd floor offers a panoramic view of the city and on clear days you can see as far as the Gulf of Mexico. There are free guided tours lasting 45 minutes on the hour. The Visitors Info Center on the plaza level is open 08:00–17:00 weekdays.

Near the New Capitol, two blocks west on S Bronough Street, is the **Museum of Florida History** where recovered Spanish treasure vies for attention with prehistoric finds. War relics, a steamboat and space shuttles complete the collection. Open 09:00–16:30 Monday–Friday, 10:00–16:30 Saturday, noon–16:30 Sunday and holidays.

Further north on neighbouring N Adams Street is the Georgian-style **Governor's Mansion**. Its state rooms are filled with fine antiques and gifts from abroad. Only five rooms are open to the public, tours of which are available during legislative session and Christmas holidays. Call tel: (904) 488-4661 for times.

Museums and Archaeological Sites *

Head out of the downtown area on E Park Avenue to the **Knott House Museum**, built by a free Black builder in 1843, which today houses a large collection of gilt-framed mirrors. Rhymes written on silk ribbons by its eccentric owner are attached to the furniture. This was the site of the formal declaration of emancipation of North Florida slaves in 1865, officially freeing all remaining slaves in the state.

The city is just a few miles from America's greatest concentration of plantations – 71 estates along the road between Tallahassee and Thomasville, Georgia.

WALKABOUT

Tallahassee has at least three easy walking routes to take in the main sights. The downtown area is also served by a free trolley. Free walking and trolley maps are available at the **Tallahassee Area Visitor Information Center**, New Capitol Building.
Downtown: start from the New Capitol for a taste of the city as political and retail centre with varied architecture and shopping.
Park Avenue Historic District Tour: explore the city's historic churches, old cemetery and the parks which were once a dirt clearing to protect the city from attack.
Calhoun Street Historic District Tour: has the largest concentration of historic homes and was once known as Gold Dust Street, due to its many wealthy residents.

Above: St Mark's light-house was built with stone from a 17th-century fort.

SOUTH FROM TALLAHASSEE

A Spanish mission and 17th-century fort made **St Marks** a powerful place. Stones from the fort were used to build a lighthouse which is still in operation today. A later Civil War fort here was separately occupied by each of the opposing sides. Once the third-largest cotton port on the Gulf Coast, nearby **Apalachicola** served as a base for blockade runners during the Civil War. It is now the state's most important oyster fishery – and home to the John Gorrie State Museum, dedicated to the man who invented fridges, ice-makers and air conditioners.
To the north and west is the **Apalachicola National Forest** and the **Torreya State Park**, named after the rare 'torreya' tree which is said to have grown in the garden of Eden.

On a hill to the west of town near the intersection of Tennessee Street and W Mission Road lies the **San Luis Archaeological and Historic Site**, home of Apalachee Indians and Spanish settlers from 1656 to 1704. An annual heritage festival includes costumed re-enactments and there are also regular excavations around the 50-acre (20ha) plot. Another historical re-enactment takes place at the **De Soto Archaeological Site** off Lafayette Street, the place where Hernando de Soto and his troops celebrated the first Christmas in America, back in 1539.

The **Tallahassee Museum of History and Natural Science** on Museum Drive has native red wolves, Florida panthers and alligators living on 52 acres (21ha) alongside an 1880s farm exhibit and a plantation home.

State Parks **

Tallahassee is surrounded by numerous state parks, including the **Florida Caverns State Park** near Marianna, which provides hourly tours through caves and caverns filled with spectacular calcite formations: soda straws, stalactites, stalagmites, columns, flowstones and draperies. Open 08:00–sunset daily.

The **Torreya State Park** is the site of Gregory House, a former cotton plantation; the surrounding park is filled with the rare torreya evergreen, as well as yew trees and the US champion-winged elm. Open 08:00–sunset daily, house tours 10:00 Monday–Friday, and 10:00, 14:00, 16:00 on Saturday and Sunday.

The **Apalachicola National Forest** includes more than 500,000 acres (202,347ha) of untouched native forest and lies just 10 miles (17km) south of the city. Tallahassee is also surrounded by lakes, among them Lake Jackson, Lake Bradford and Lake Talquin.

SOUTH TO CEDAR KEY

Fifty miles (80km) out of Tallahassee you reach the inland town of **Perry**, once famed for its logging production. The **Forest Capital State Museum** has an authentic 'Cracker' farm, a homestead typical of this area.

Hickory Mound Impoundment west of Perry offers canoeing, hiking and cycling trails. Call tel: (904) 838-1306 to check the hunting season dates, when the area is closed.

South of Perry the US98 runs down to Cedar Key. Stop off at **Keaton Beach** or **Steinhatchee** on the way; both with numerous bars and seafood restaurants overlooking the Gulf – excellent places to relax and watch the sun set.

A few miles south on US98, turn right down Highway 349 to reach the **Manatee Springs State Park**, where a spring spills out an average 116.9 million gallons (532 million litres) of water daily. Manatees can be spotted here, and watersports enthusiasts are well catered for; there are also picnic areas.

The springs feed the **Suwannee River** which flows for more than 200 miles (322km) across Florida from the Okefenokee Swamp in Georgia. At the mouth of the river, the town of Suwannee is a good place to hire a houseboat for a few days, or take a boat trip into the Gulf for the day.

Along the stretch of coastline known as **Big Bend**, swamps, riverlets and islands take over. Charming **Cedar Key**, at the end of Route 24, lies on an island at the outer limit of the marshes. Once a thriving port, the village lost importance as ships grew too large for the shallow waters, but much of its shipping history – plus a fine shell collection – is displayed in the **Cedar Key State Museum**. Call tel: (904) 543-5350 for opening times. **Cedar Key Scrub Reserve** provides 4000 acres (1619ha) of marsh habitat for seabirds, manatees, eagles, and even black bears.

WAKULLA SPRINGS

Wakulla is a native American word meaning 'mysterious waters', an apt title for this wilderness area, 12 miles (19km) south of Tallahassee. Virtually untouched, the area was the setting for Tarzan movies in the 1930s. Today glass-bottom boats take visitors over the 'bottomless' springs which are said to be among the deepest in the world – it is still a mystery exactly how deep. Scuba divers can venture into the depths, while boat tours afford a glimpse of alligators, snakes and numerous birds – some 154 species have been spotted in the area.

Below: *Heed the warning signs at the Apalachicola National Forest.*

The Northwest at a Glance

BEST TIMES TO VISIT

Unlike most of Florida, the Northwest experiences little seasonal fluctuation. With water temperatures around 70°F (21°C) and air temperatures of 74°F (23°C), the region is **pleasant** all **year-round**.

GETTING THERE

No direct flights from Europe service this area as yet, but the **regional airports** at Tallahassee, Pensacola, Fort Walton/Okaloosa County and Panama City receive connecting flights from the major United States carriers. **Taxis** and hotel **shuttle buses** are the main mode of transport from and to the airports. **Road** connections to the Northwest area are good. **Interstate 10** (I10) runs east–west from Tallahassee to Pensacola. **Highway 85** goes south, from I10 to Fort Walton Beach, which is also accessible from Pensacola, along **Highway 98**. Panama City is reached from I10 south along **Highway 231**. **Train** connections are difficult, but **Greyhound buses** run to this coast from Alabama and from Georgia.

GETTING AROUND

The major **car rental** companies have desks at the airports and in downtown locations. Local **buses** and shuttle buses run along the beach in Panama City Beach but only during daylight hours.

WHERE TO STAY

Pensacola Beach
LUXURY
Dunes, 333 Ft Pickens Rd, tel: (904) 932-3536. On the beach, offers a putting green and golf packages.

MID-RANGE
Five Flags Inn, 299 Ft Pickens Rd, tel: (904) 932-3586. Facing the Gulf.

BUDGET
Beachside Resort and Conference Center, 16 Via De Luna Drive, tel: (904) 932-5331.

Panama City Beach
LUXURY
Bay Point Yacht and Country Club, 3900 Marriott Dr, tel: (904) 235-6966. Spacious golf resort.

MID-RANGE
Holiday Inn Sunspree Resort, 1127 Front Beach Road, tel: (904) 234-1111. Good for families.

BUDGET
The Florida Palms Motel, 17784 Front Beach Rd, tel: (904) 233-1136. Self-catering units opposite the beach.

Tallahassee
LUXURY
Sheraton Tallahassee Hotel, 101 S Adams St, tel: (904) 224-5000, fax: 224-1168. Good location in the city centre.

MID-RANGE
Radisson Hotel Tallahassee, 415 N Monroe St, tel: (904) 224-6000, fax: 224-6000, ext. 4118. In downtown area.

BUDGET
Best Western, 2016 Apalachee Parkway, tel: (904) 656-6312, toll free: 800 827-7390. Within walking distance of the centre of town.

WHERE TO EAT

The long shoreline contributes to a love of seafood. Panacea claims to be the blue crab capital of the world and Apalachicola oysters are justifiably famous.

Pensacola Beach
Boy on a Dolphin, 400 Pensacola Beach, tel: (904) 932-7954. Famous for fresh seafood and steaks.
Flounder's Chowder & Ale House, Pensacola Beach, tel: (904) 932-2003. Award-winning seafood, great desserts.
Jamie's, 424 E Zaragoza St, Pensacola downtown, tel: (904) 434-2911. French food in Seville Square.

Panama City Beach
Billy's, 3000 Thomas Drive, tel: (904) 235-2349. Good seafood but closes at 21:00.
Boar's Head, 17290 Front Beach Road, tel: (904) 234-6628. Another award-winner, best known for its prime rib; high prices but worth it.

The Northwest at a Glance

The Treasure Ship,
3605 Thomas Drive, tel: (904)
234-8881. Good for children,
discounted dining between
16:30 and 18:00.

Tallahassee
Andrew's Second Act,
228 S Adams St, tel:
222-3444. Award-winner;
reservations are advised.
Barnacle Bill's, 1830 N
Monroe St, tel: 385-8734.
Excellent seafood.
**Nicholson Farmhouse
restaurant**, 15 miles (24km)
north of Tallahassee, tel:
539-5931. Excellent Cajun
country cooking; take your
own wine along.

Pensacola
Cordova Mall, 5100 N Ninth
Ave, tel: (904) 477-5563.
**Ninth Avenue Antique
Mall**, 380 N Ninth Ave, tel:
(904) 438-3961. Antique
shops and bric-a-brac.
University Mall,
7171 N Davis Highway,
tel: (904) 478-3600.
Seville Square, restored buil-
dings, gift and antique shops.

Tallahassee
Governor's Square, 1500
Apalachee Parkway, tel:
671-INFO. Largest selection
of speciality shops in the area.
Village Commons,
1400 Village Square Blvd, tel:
(904) 413-9200. Upmarket
speciality shops mixed with
factory discount stores.

Downtown Havana,
12 miles (19km) north of
Tallahassee in historic quarter
of Havana. Art galleries,
cafés and speciality shops.

Gulf Coast Excursions,
tel: (904) 984-5895.
Reservations for group or
self-guided tours of the
many different waterways.
Lake Talquin Tours,
tel: (904) 877-3198. Fishing
trips and party cruises.
**Wakulla Springs Twilight
Cruise and Dinner**,
tel: (904) 922-3633.
Monthly dinner in the historic
Wakulla Springs Lodge and a
moonlight cruise on the river.

**Emerald Coast Convention
and Visitors Bureau**,
1540 Hwy 98 East, Fort
Walton Beach, FL32548,
tel: (904) 651-7131,
fax: 651-7149.
Historic Pensacola,
120 Church St, Pensacola,
FL32501, tel: (904) 444-8905,
fax: 444-8641.
**Pensacola Convention and
Visitors Bureau**, 1401 E

Gregory St, Pensacola,
FL32501, tel: (904)
434-1234, fax: 432-8211.
**Panama City Beach
Convention and Visitor
Bureau**, 12015 W Front
Beach Road, Panama City
Beach, FL32417, tel: (904)
233-6503, fax: 233-5072.
**Tallahassee Area Conven-
tion and Visitor Bureau**,
200 W College Ave, Talla-
hassee, FL32301, tel: (904)
413-9200, fax: 487-4621.

Diving
Diver's Den, 3120 Thomas
Drive, Panama City Beach,
tel: (904) 234-8717.
The Scuba Shop,
348 Miracle Strip Parkway,
Fort Walton Beach,
tel: (904) 243-3373.

Golf
Emerald Bay Golf Club,
4001 Emerald Coast Parkway,
Fort Walton Beach,
tel: (904) 837-4455.
Signal Hill Golf Course,
9615 Thomas Drive, Panama
City, tel: (904) 234-3218.
The Moor Golf Club,
3220 Avalon Blvd, Pensacola,
tel: (904) 995-GOLF (4653).

PENSACOLA	J	F	M	A	M	J	J	A	S	O	N	D
AVERAGE TEMP. °F	53	55	60	67	74	80	81	81	78	70	60	54
AVERAGE TEMP. °C	12	13	16	20	23	27	27	27	26	21	16	12
HOURS OF SUN DAILY	12	13	12	13	13	14	14	14	13	12	12	12
RAINFALL in	4.5	4.5	5.5	4.5	3.5	5	7	7.5	6	4	4	4.5
RAINFALL mm	109	117	137	109	96	129	177	193	152	99	94	112
DAYS OF RAINFALL	9	9	10	10	9	11	12	13	12	9	9	8

7
The West Coast

Hostile natives and submerged reefs guarding many insect-infested swamps once saw this area frequented only by buccaneers in search of a hide out. Florida's West Coast is relatively new territory for European visitors too, but beaches, resort areas, private islands, and a wealth of culture have started attracting tourists.

What Flagler did for the east coast in terms of development, magnate **Henry Plant** achieved here on the West Coast. Many elegant Victorian homes in Tampa and along the coastal strip owe their origins to Plant, who brought the railroad and, with it, industry and wealth.

Tampa lies at the heart of the West Coast development, characterized by its industrial history, port and tourist attractions. Nearby ethnic enclaves add their own inimitable style to the region; a Czech community in Brooksville holds regular strudel bakes in an effort to retain the ways of their fatherland.

St Petersburg has stunning beaches and spectacular sunsets. A string of islands leads down to **Sarasota**, where classical music mixes with the razzmatazz of the circus. The West Coast even has its own **Venice** – criss-crossed with canals and home to the world's only clown college.

Further down the coast wildlife replaces city glitz as the main attraction, with **Fort Myers** and **Naples** surrounded by national parks and the vast **Everglades**. Many Americans have bought homes in this area, making it as rich and exclusive as its east coast counterpart, Palm Beach. Visitors always receive a warm welcome, whether driving through on a day trip or staying awhile.

Don't Miss

*** Sunshine Skyway: enjoy the views of the islands and Tampa Bay.
*** Busch Gardens: thrill of roller coasters tempered with wildlife and gardens.
*** Ybor City: Cuban life, history and entertainment.
** Corkscrew Swamp Sanctuary: a wilderness of 11,000 acres (4452ha), inhabited by alligators, bobcats and otters.
** John and Mable Ringling complex: amazing combination put together by this famous circus couple.

Opposite: *Fun in the sun at Tigertail Beach on Marco Island.*

TAMPA BAY AND SURROUNDS
Tampa *

Native Americans first discovered the natural attractions of Tampa, its harbour protected by the sandbanks of St Petersburg. **Hernando de Soto** was the first European known to have set foot here (1539) – in search of gold; the area remained largely undeveloped for the next 200 years. First called Fort Brooke, the town became Tampa in 1855, named after the Indian word for 'sticks of fire'. Thirty years later, **Don Vicente Martinez Ybor** moved his cigar factory from Key West to Tampa, not only building a world-renowned industry here, but also forming the base of the city's thriving Hispanic community. Cubans followed the cigar maker in droves and it was only the strict US sanctions against Cuban tobacco that brought a stop to an industry employing some 12,000 people. Today **Ybor City** remains one of the most vibrant areas of Tampa with excellent restaurants and lively nightlife as well as colourful markets.

The heart of the beautifully restored Ybor City is the former cigar factory, **Ybor Square**, which is now an attractive shopping mall with many speciality stores, antique shops and ethnic restaurants. The **Old Hyde Park Village** is another restored section of the city, and is filled with upmarket shops, pavement cafés and chic restaurants.

West Coast

Left: Spanish and Cuban restaurants are a must in downtown Ybor City.
Below: *Riding the Python at Busch Gardens is only for the brave.*

BUSCH GARDENS

The latest attraction at Busch Gardens is a ninth themed area, **Egypt**, where bazaars and entertainers abound. Explore King Tutankhamen's tomb, but don't miss Montu, the world's largest roller coaster with an inverted loop at 104ft (31m) and a peak G-force of 3.85. Other themed areas are the **Congo**, **Morocco**, **Nairobi**, **Serengeti Plain**, **Crown Colony**, **Stanleyville**, **Bird Gardens** and **Timbuktu**.

The skyscraper area downtown is home to the **Tampa Museum of Art** on N Ashley Drive. Seven galleries house Greek and Roman antiquities along with some of the finest exhibitions in the state. Dedicated to **African–American art**, the museum on N Marion Street was the first of its kind in Florida and is famed for its Barnett–Aden collection.

Children may prefer the **Museum of Science and Industry** (MOSI) on 4801 E Fowler Avenue. The planetarium, space simulators and hurricane chamber are both educational and fun. There's also the Butterfly Encounter (walk-through cages filled with butterflies) and an Omni Theater with a 360° revolving dome. Open 09:00–16:30 Sunday–Thursday in autumn and winter, 09:00–18:00 Sunday–Thursday and 09:00–21:00 Friday–Saturday in spring and summer.

Tampa has its share of theme parks, from **Adventure Island**, offering speed slides and other water attractions, to **Buccaneer Bay** with yet more sensational water rides in a natural spring setting.

The **Florida Aquarium** at Garrison Seaport Center covers 152,000ft^2 (14,121m^2) and houses 4350 species of fish, animal and plant, while **Lowry Park Zoo** on 7530 N Boulevard has a manatee treatment tank that doubles as an emergency rescue clinic.

St Petersburg **

The long, wide and white sand beaches of **St Petersburg** and neighbouring **Clearwater** have made this area a family favourite. Both cities lie on the thin Pinellas peninsula that protects Tampa Bay, with 28 miles (45km) of pristine beaches bordering the Gulf of Mexico on its western side.

The Guinness Book of Records credits the area with the longest run of **sunny days** ever recorded – 768 days, from 9 February 1967 to 17 March 1969. Until 1986 the local newspaper was given away for free on rainy days – something that happened on average four times a year.

The Pinellas coast is lined with attractions, shopping malls, marinas and restaurants. One nine-block area of St Petersburg's downtown is being renovated to satisfy the demands of any shopaholic. Another, **Tyrone Square**, already has more than 150 shops including four department stores. Antique buyers should head to **Antique Alley** on 4th Street North, the Antique Arcade on Central Avenue, and **The Pier** on 2nd Avenue near the Museum of Fine Arts, a five-storey market filled with shops and entertainment overlooking the water.

For those rare rainy days, St Petersburg offers the **Florida International Museum** on 2nd Street, with travelling exhibitions of art and antiquities, as well as the world's greatest collection of works by Salvador Dali located at the **Salvador Dali Museum** on 3rd Street.

Below: *Fabulous St Pete Beach, a good place to be on a hot day.*

The city is also home to **Great Explorations: The Hands On Museum**, with many interactive exhibits to fascinate adults and children alike, such as the Hall of Mirrors, neon tubes that glow when touched and puzzles. Open 10:00–17:00 Monday–Saturday, noon–17:00 on Sunday. Closed over Christmas and Thanksgiving.

The **Sunken Gardens** on nearby 1875 N Fourth Street holds a lush, exotic collection of over 50,000 tropical plants (including fantastic orchids), animals and birds. There are also regular parrot shows.

Visitors to St Petersburg should not leave without a drive across the toll bridge, the **Sunshine Skyway** that leads down to Sarasota and affords magnificent views across Tampa Bay and the islands.

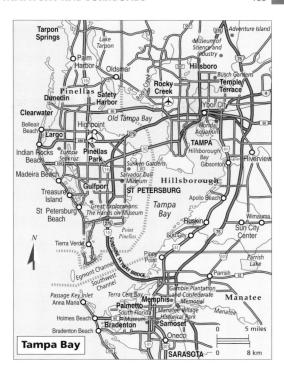

Tampa Bay

Pinellas Peninsula ★★

Take a drive up Gulf Boulevard past the many beaches and resorts, stopping off at John's Pass Village **Madeira Beach**, an old-time fishing village with shops and seafood restaurants overlooking the water. The Suncoast Seabird Sanctuary at **Indian Shores**, a nonprofit refuge for birds and the largest bird hospital in the United States, is also worth a stop. Open 09:00–dusk daily.

Clearwater to the north has attractions of its own, including the family-oriented **Celebration Station** on US19 which offers a variety of exciting rides, as well as mini golf, go-karting and bumper boats. A harbour dinner cruise aboard the **Admiral Dinner Boat** is an unforgettably romantic experience.

The **Clearwater Marine Science Center Aquarium** on Windward Passage specializes in education, and rehabilitates dolphins, whales and turtles, rescuing handicapped and injured animals that would otherwise not be able to survive in the wild.

WHAT NEXT?

A short monorail ride from downtown Tampa leads to the waterfront marketplace of **Harbour Island**, with unusual shops, restaurants and live entertainment. Another innovation is the **Garrison Seaport Center**, which is set to become the largest entertainment complex in the United States. The **Florida Aquarium** has already opened and a Music Amphitheatre will be added, all linked by water taxis, ferries and the **Riverwalk**.

Above: *The spotting of manatees is possible off Anna Maria Island's pier.*
Opposite: *The impressive, well-kept grounds of the John and Mable Ringling Museum in Sarasota.*

MANATEE SPOTTING

Unfortunately the sea cow population is declining, but these gentle creatures still frequent the Gulf Coast. Good places to spot them include: **Terra Ceia Bay** at Sea Breeze Point; **Snead Island Emerson Point**; **Palma Sola Bay** on the Causeway and at Rose Park; **Manatee River**; Kingfish boat ramp, Coquina Beach Park, Leffis Key and Bayfront Park, all on **Anna Maria Island**. Sightings are guaranteed at the **South Florida Museum** in Bradenton.

BRADENTON

The area was first inhabited by Timucuan Indians and, although visited by Spanish explorers, was not developed until 1842. Josiah Gates was the county's first permanent settler and **Major Robert Gamble** soon joined him. Gamble's house and huge plantation (the only surviving Antebellum plantation) can be visited on Patten Avenue in Bradenton. Open 09:00–12:00 and 13:00–17:00 daily. Guided tours 09:30, 10:30, 13:00–16:00 Thursday–Monday.

Bradenton offers small-town charm. Set inland from the Gulf of Mexico, at the mouth of the Manatee River, it proudly preserves its historical roots. **Manatee Village Historical Park**, on Manatee Avenue takes visitors back in time with its carefully restored buildings. A memorial on 75th Street is dedicated to Hernando de Soto, the first Spaniard to land here, and the **South Florida Museum, Bishop Planetarium and Parker Manatee Aquarium** on 10th Street West covers the history of Florida from the Stone Age to the Space Age.

From Bradenton you can also enjoy a 75-minute ride aboard the **Florida Gulf Coast Railroad**. Alternatively, the world's largest airboat is available for trips through the **Myakka River State Park**, a dense woodland along the Myakka River and a breeding ground for numerous birds, which lies between Bradenton and Sarasota on Highway 72. Call ahead for opening times.

SARASOTA

Sarasota considers itself the cultural capital of Florida, thanks in no small way to the influence of grand circus master **John Ringling** and his wife Mable. The city is home to the Florida West Coast Symphony and offers a marvellous host of artistic venues, such as the beautiful **Asolo Performing Arts Center** and the **Van Wezel Performing Arts Hall**.

The **Asolo Theater** is a 19th-century playhouse that was partly shipped from Asolo in Italy and was reconstructed in the United States. It is situated just up the road from **Bellm's Cars and Music of Yesterday**, which features an interesting collection of antique cars and more than 1500 musical antiques. Open 09:30–17:30 daily. The city's symphony orchestra performs regularly and there is a varied programme of fine opera and ballet productions. An annual jazz festival is held each April, as well as other community events such as the annual premier of the new circus season, dedicated to the memory of the famous Ringlings. Their Venetian-style winter home, **Ca'd'Zan**, which they designed after a visit to Europe, is open to the public and gives a taste of the wealth and glitz of the 1920s. Open 10:00–17:30 daily.

The adjacent **John and Mable Ringling Museum of Art** employs volunteer guides to take visitors around the 22-gallery maze of Old Masters and contemporary artworks, the classical courtyards adorned with statues, and Mable Ringling's fine rose garden. In honour of their circus background, the Ringlings also gave Sarasota the lovely **Circus Galleries** museum, housing gaily painted parade wagons, costumes and other circus memorabilia. Open 10:00–17:30 daily.

BARRIER ISLANDS

Egmont Key: uninhabited island in Tampa Bay, with white, sandy beaches, a large population of turtles and excellent beachcombing. **Anna Maria Island:** a 7-mile (11km) island with a distinctly laid-back Caribbean feel. **Longboat Key:** tennis and golf are the main attractions on this upmarket island, which also holds the Mote Marine Aquarium and Pelican Man's Bird Sanctuary. **Lido and St Armands Keys:** resort area with glitzy shops and restaurants. **Siesta Key:** powdery sand and Point Rock, which is known for sponges, colourful shells and tropical fish.

MARCO ISLAND

Marco Island, 16 miles (26km) south of Naples, is the largest and only developed island of the Ten Thousand Island chain that runs down to the Florida Keys. Take a **trolley tour** to explore the island, dine out in one of the many excellent seafood restaurants or shop in the quaint old-style shopping centres. Indian burial mounds and a history of providing sanctuary for pirates gives the island plenty of folklore – and promise of buried treasure.

FORT MYERS

Fort Myers, developed during the Indian wars, started to grow in the late 1880s when tourists began to flock in.

The Edison and Ford Homes **

Among the first arrivals was **Thomas Edison** who built a retreat on McGregor Boulevard. The house is now a fascinating museum displaying hundreds of his inventions (some of the original light bulbs still burn). Tours only: 09:00–17:30 Monday–Saturday, noon–17:30 Sunday. Next door is Henry Ford's winter home, **Mangoes**. You can buy combination tickets to see both museums.

A few streets away is the **Fort Myers Historical Museum** with an interesting collection of Calusa Indian artefacts and Ethel Cooper glass. Parked outside is the *Esperanza*, longest and last of the Pullman coaches.

North of town lies the **Babcock Wilderness Adventure**, where you can join a 90-minute swamp-buggy tour and see bison, alligators, panthers, wild turkey and deer.

Below: *The Castaways Beach Plantation on Sanibel Island.*

Sanibel *

Explore the **JN 'Ding' Darling National Wildlife Refuge**, where there is a five-mile (8km) drive through mangrove swamps as well as walkways and canoe trails. Sanibel Island has five public beaches and the **Bailey-Matthews Shell Museum** (3075 Sanibel-Captiva Road), which holds about two million land and sea shells. Open 10:00–16:00 Tuesday-Sunday. Enthusiasts eager to collect their own may pick only dead shells on the beaches of Sanibel and Captiva. The best area is reputed to be the 'shell line', where the highest waves break on the beach. Please take note that a law introduced in 1995 strictly prohibits the gathering of live specimens.

AROUND NAPLES

The city of Naples is really the main resort area of this wonderful stretch of the coast. It lies between the Gulf of Mexico and the Everglades, right at the northern tip of the **Ten Thousand Island** chain that runs down to the Florida Keys. Only **Marco Island** is developed.

Naples *

Naples itself has little to offer in the way of museums or attractions, though the surrounding country has a wealth of places to explore. One exception in the

city is the **Collier County Museum** which displays the history of the region from prehistoric to modern times.

The **Teddy Bear Museum** of Naples, on 2511 Pine Ridge Road, features a collection of more than 3000 lovable cuddly furry toys from around the world, displayed in a variety of novel poses.

The **Philharmonic Center for the Arts**, situated on Pelican Bay Boulevard, is the regional hub for the arts and music with four art galleries and two sculpture gardens, as well as a full yearly programme of events.

Sanctuaries **

To explore the peaceful surrounding countryside, visit the **Conservancy's Naples Nature Center** on 1450 Merrihue Drive, where there are aquariums and a serpentarium. Boat tours are available from here. Or you can head 20 miles (32km) north of Naples to the **Corkscrew Swamp Sanctuary** where alligators, bobcats and otters live among giant bald cypress trees several hundreds of years old. The teeming birdlife will delight novices and ornithologists alike, and is best observed in winter when the birds tend to flock around the remaining pools of water.

Above: *Idyllic sands and sea in the Fort Myers area.*

BARRIER ISLANDS

Boca Grande: a retreat for the rich who enjoy its 19th-century atmosphere of wooden houses and sleepy fishing village.
Cabbage Key: a Calusa Indian shell mound lies under an inn built by playwright Mary Roberts Rinehart.
Sanibel: one-third of the island is dedicated to the **JN 'Ding' Darling National Wildlife Refuge**, named after a Pulitzer prize-winning cartoonist; shell-collecting here is exceptional.
Gasparilla: was once a favourite pirate haven.
Captiva: very popular among shell-seekers.

The West Coast at a Glance

BEST TIMES TO VISIT

Locals pride themselves on the **360 days** of **sunshine** this region receives annually. Temperatures rarely fall below 60°F (15°C). In mid-summer 90°F (32°C) is common, but tempered by cool sea breezes. Near the **Everglades** it is rainy and humid in summer, with swarms of mosquitoes.

GETTING THERE

Tampa International Airport is rapidly expanding to cope with demand from Europe. It also has good United States connections. The **Sarasota–Bradenton International Airport** is well serviced by American carriers. **Southwest Florida Regional Airport** serves the Fort Myers area. Major **car rental** companies are represented at convenient locations, and hotels operate airport **shuttle buses**. By car the West Coast is accessible off **Interstate 75** which runs north–south and from **Interstate 4** which heads west from Daytona Beach and Orlando. **Highway 19** hugs the coast from Tallahassee down to St Petersburg, while **Highway 41** runs down to Naples. From Miami the **Tamiami Trail** runs west to Naples, while the **Everglades Parkway** connects Naples with Fort Lauderdale. **Greyhound** offers a good interstate service stopping in Tampa, St Petersburg, Sarasota and Fort Myers.

GETTING AROUND

Road networks are good and it is easy to cross the state to Orlando and the theme parks or down to the Everglades. The cities all have local **bus** networks (essential in Tampa where tourist attractions are generally beyond walking distance of each other). Clearwater and Fort Myers have **trolley services,** and **ferries** operate between the islands.

WHERE TO STAY

Tampa
LUXURY
Saddlebrook Resort, 100 Saddlebrook Way, tel: (813) 973-1111. North of the city.

MID-RANGE
Holiday Inn Tampa Busch Gardens, 2701 E Fowler Ave, tel: (813) 971-4710, fax: 977-0153. Close to theme park.

St Petersburg
LUXURY
Don CeSar Beach Resort, 3400 Gulf Blvd, St Pete Beach, tel: (813) 360-1881, fax: 367-3609. Used by F Scott Fitzgerald and Al Capone.

MID-RANGE
The Colonial Gateway Inn, 6300 Gulf Blvd, St Pete Beach, tel: (813) 367-2711, fax: 367-7068.

BUDGET
Inn on the Beach, 1401 Gulf Way, St Pete Beach, tel: (813) 360-8844, fax: 894-3339.

Clearwater area
LUXURY
Innisbrook Hilton Resort, PO Drawer 1088, Tarpon Springs, tel: (813) 942-2000, fax: 942-5578. Expensive golfing resort.

MID-RANGE
Best Western Sea Wake Inn, 691 S Gulfview Blvd, Clearwater Beach, tel: (813) 443-7652, fax: 461-2836. On the beach.

BUDGET
Chart House Hotel, 850 Bay Way Blvd, Clearwater Beach, tel: (813) 449-8007, fax: 443-6081. Overlooks the bay.

Sarasota area
LUXURY
Hyatt Sarasota, 100 Blvd of the Arts, tel: (813) 366-9000, fax: 952-1987. Located in the city centre; some rooms overlook the bay.

MID-RANGE
Five Oaks Bed and Breakfast Inn, 1102 Riverside Drive, Palmetto, tel: (813) 723-1236. Listed in the National Historic Register, former Sears Roebuck home.

Naples
LUXURY
LaPlaya Beach and Racquet Inn, 9891 Gulf Shore Blvd, tel: (941) 597-3123, fax: 597-6278. Newly renovated hotel, targeting golfers and honeymooners.

The West Coast at a Glance

The Registry Resort, 475 Seagate Drive, tel: (941) 597-3232, fax: 597-7168. Luxury resort with a shuttle through mangroves to the beach.

MID-RANGE
Vanderbilt Beach Motel, 9225 Gulfshore Drive, tel: (941) 597-3144, fax: 597-2199. Beachfront motel with dock and boat ramp.

BUDGET
Trail's End Motel, Tamiami Trail, tel: (941) 262-6336. Clean and comfortable.

WHERE TO EAT

Tampa
Colombia Restaurant, 2117 E 7th Ave, Ybor City, tel: (813) 248-4961. Claims to be America's oldest Spanish restaurant, created to serve Cuban cigar makers.
Café Creole, 1330 Ninth Avenue, Ybor City, tel: (813) 247-6283. Cajun delicacies.

St Petersburg
Hurricane, 9th Ave & Gulf Way, tel: (813) 360-9558. Very casual, but reservations are advised.
Wine Cellar, 17307 Gulf Blvd, N Redington Beach, tel: (831) 393-3491. International menu, highly acclaimed.

Clearwater
Calico Jack's, Adam Mark Caribbean Resort, tel: (813) 443-5714. Caribbean food and great sunsets.

Jimmy Hall's Steakhouse, 515 Hendricks St, tel: (813) 446-3151. Huge steaks and good seafood.

Sarasota area
Cha Cha Coconuts, St Armands Circle, tel: (813) 388-3300. Caribbean food mixed with US treats.
Hemingways, 325 John Ringling Blvd, Lido Beach, tel: (813) 388-3948. Popular steak, seafood and pasta place.

Naples
Maxwells on the Bay, Venetian Village, 4300 Gulf Shore Blvd, tel: (941) 263-1662. Elegant restaurant with affordable prices.
Sign of the Vine, 980 Solana Road, tel: (941) 261-6745. Elegance and good food.

SHOPPING

Gulf Coast Factory Shops, 5461 Factory Shops Blvd, Bradenton, tel: (813) 723-1150. Designer gear at a fraction of the retail price.
Red Barn Flea Market, 1701 1st St East, Bradenton, tel: (813) 747-3794. Explore over 700 booths and stalls.

Tarpon Springs. Greek arts and crafts in Main Street.
Shell Factory, 2787 N Tamiami Trail, North Fort Myers, tel: (941) 995-2141.

TOURS AND EXCURSIONS

Big Rad Balloon, Fantasy Flights Inc, 16302 E Course Drive, Tampa, tel: (813) 969-4381.
Marina Jack II Dinner Boat, 2 Marina Plaza, Sarasota, tel: (941) 366-9255. Cruises around lovely Sarasota Bay.

USEFUL CONTACTS

Tampa/Hillsborough Convention and Visitors Association, 111 Madison St, Suite 1010, Tampa, tel: (813) 223-2752, fax: 229-6616.
St Petersburg/Clearwater Area Convention and Visitors Bureau, 1 Stadium Drive, St Petersburg, tel: (813) 582-7892, fax: 582-7949.
Bradenton Area Convention and Visitors Bureau, tel: (941) 729-9177, fax: 729-1820.
Sarasota Convention and Visitors Bureau, 655 N Tamiami Trail, tel: (941) 957-1877, fax: 951-2956.

TAMPA	J	F	M	A	M	J	J	A	S	O	N	D
AVERAGE TEMP. °F	60	62	66	71	77	81	82	82	81	75	68	62
AVERAGE TEMP. °C	16	17	19	22	25	27	28	28	27	24	20	17
HOURS OF SUN DAILY	12	12	12	13	13	14	14	14	13	12	12	12
RAINFALL in	2	3	3	1	3	5	7	8	6	2	2	2
RAINFALL mm	51	76	76	25	76	127	178	203	152	51	51	51
DAYS OF RAINFALL	7	8	8	7	9	13	14	12	11	9	7	7

8
The Florida Keys

The Florida Keys and Key West, to give the area its correct name, is an approximately 180-mile (290km) chain of islands trailing off Florida's southeastern tip and arcing to the southwest into the Atlantic. The northernmost island of **Key Largo** is the land base for the **John Pennekamp Coral Reef Marine Park**. The most southerly point, the **Dry Tortugas**, lies just about 85 miles (137km) north of Havana, Cuba.

An official count for the number of islands is unavailable, but estimates put the total at around 800, spread over 2700 sq miles (6995km²) of coral reefs. Forty-two of the islands are linked by the 113 mile (182km) US1, or **Overseas Highway**, which spans 43 bridges including the famous **Seven Mile Bridge**.

Despite the road link, most of the islands are accessible only by water. This has ensured that the region is able to preserve a feeling of the past; today all the islands are protected by the **Florida Keys National Marine Sanctuary**. Fishing, sunning and snorkelling are still the main activities and nightlife is limited to eating out and sampling the different bars. The atmosphere is unlike that in any other part of Florida – this could easily be the Caribbean, rather than the United States.

One of this region's most famous residents, author **Ernest Hemingway**, has come to epitomize the lifestyle of the Keys, and little has changed since he lived, wrote and fished here – except for the growing number of visitors who head south to try and capture the spirit of these beguiling, laid-back islands.

DON'T MISS

*** **The Dolphin Research Center**, **Grassy Key:** inspired the popular movie *Flipper*.
** **The Wrecker's Museum**, **Key West:** pirate mementos, and marine artefacts.
** **Mallory Square**, **Key West:** admire the sunset.
** **John Pennekamp State Park**, **Key Largo:** first underwater state park; America's only living coral reef.
* ***African Queen***, **Key Largo:** original boat used by Humphrey Bogart and Katharine Hepburn in the movie *African Queen*.

Opposite: *Underwater adventures abound in the Florida Keys.*

KEY LARGO

The largest island in the chain at nearly 30 miles (48km) long, Key Largo is also the most developed. Key Largo claims to be the **diving capital** of the USA and, while this title might be disputed by some, there's no doubt the place is popular with divers. The **John Pennekamp Coral Reef State Park** was the first underwater sanctuary in America, established in order to protect part of the only living coral reef in the United States. It covers 53,661 acres (21,716ha) of submerged land and 2350 acres (951ha) above water. Visitors can enjoy a full range of watersports and sightseeing activities. The wonderland of 500 species of fish and 55 varieties of coral is also accessible to non-swimmers via glass-bottom boats.

Land-based attractions include the **Crocodile Lakes National Wildlife Refuge** and the original *African Queen* steamboat, which featured in a film starring Humphrey Bogart and Katharine Hepburn. The boat has been fully restored and now rests at the Key Largo Harbor Marina. There's also the 1951 Chris-Craft, used as a prop in the film *On Golden Pond*, again starring Katharine Hepburn alongside veteran actor Henry Fonda.

In historical Tavernier, the station, churches and pioneer homes date back to the turn of the century.

CLIMATE

Winter (December–April) lows average 65°–70°F (18°–21°C). **Summer** (July–October) is **hot** and **humid** with highs around 90°F (32°C). **Hurricane season** is from **August–October** with storms most likely in late August and September.

Florida Keys

THE UPPER KEYS
Windley Key **

After passing through **Plantation Key**, named for its many tropical fruit farms, you reach **Windley Key** and the **Theater of the Sea**. Here you can see dolphins, even swim alongside them (by prior appointment, for the over-13s, and only after a 30-minute orientation crash course), or meet a live shark. There is a 'bottomless' boat to ride, as well as entertaining dolphin and sea lion shows. A new attraction is the **Trainer for a Day** programme which includes three hours of caring for and feeding the dolphins, with lessons on anatomy, physiology and dolphin behaviour. Open 09:30–16:00 daily.

The **Hurricane Memorial** at MM82 (Mile Marker 82) marks the mass grave of 423 construction workers who lost their lives during the 1935 Labor Day hurricane. **Windley Key Fossil Reef Geological Site** at MM85.3 offers free tours of a 30-acre (12ha) area of pristine hummocks, fauna and archaeological sites.

Islamorada *

Billed as the **sport fishing capital** of the world, this is the perfect base for deep-sea fishing expeditions. Marlin, tuna and dolphin (a fish – also called *mahi-mahi* – and not the mammal) are found just offshore in the Atlantic, while tarpon and bonefish offer shallow-water challenges.

Admiring without catching is possible thanks to numerous dive and snorkel charters on the island.

At **Treasure Village,** on Old Highway, you can examine salvaged treasures and browse through shops and galleries. South of Islamorada lies Long Key and the lovely **Long Key State Recreation Area**, a place to relax, fish, swim, go canoeing or walking. Book ahead for the camping facilities, particularly in peak season.

DIVING SURPRISES

The Keys are famed for their excellent scuba diving within a few miles of the shore – and for some odd underwater surprises, like the 10ft (3m) **Christ of the Deep** statue. Submerged in 25ft (8m) of water, the statue is guarded by barracuda and a wealth of coral fish. It was a gift to the Underwater Society of America from an Italian dive equipment manufacturer and is a smaller copy of the Christ of the Abysses that lies submerged off the town of Genoa in Italy. Weirder still is the **Jules Undersea Lodge**, where guests stay in a two-room lodge some 30ft (9m) underwater. It is hugely popular and you need to book at least a year in advance.

Opposite: *The Christ of the Deep, 25ft (8m) underwater at John Pennekamp Coral Reef State Park.*
Below: *Idyllic island life on Upper Matecumba Key.*

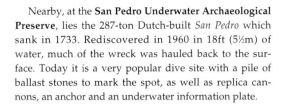

Nearby, at the **San Pedro Underwater Archaeological Preserve**, lies the 287-ton Dutch-built *San Pedro* which sank in 1733. Rediscovered in 1960 in 18ft (5½m) of water, much of the wreck was hauled back to the surface. Today it is a very popular dive site with a pile of ballast stones to mark the spot, as well as replica cannons, an anchor and an underwater information plate.

Marathon *

Before reaching Marathon, at MM59 on Grassy Key is the **Dolphin Research Center**, which works with universities and research facilities around the world. Here too, you can swim with the dolphins but need to book well ahead (at least a month before your intended visit). This was once the site of Flipper's Sea School for training dolphins and here the original 1950s *Flipper* movie was filmed.

Marathon itself has a new(ish) airport which is likely to boost the number of visitors to this area considerably. The town is also home to the **Crane Point Hammock**, an archaeological site with finds dating back some seven

centuries, and the oldest example of Conch-style architecture outside of Key West. The **Museum of Natural History** endeavours to bring the area's history to life with the help of some interesting dioramas.

Driving south from Marathon, you cross the famous **Seven Mile Bridge** which actually measures only 6.9 miles (11km), was completed in 1982 at a cost of US$45 million and is the world's longest segmental bridge. Every April, runners gather in Marathon for a special bridge race. At MM47 lies the pedestrian entrance to the **Old Seven Mile Bridge**. The structure is listed on the National Register of Historic Places and, across the Middle to Lower Keys, it rests on 546 concrete pillars.

THE LOWER KEYS

The area from Seven Mile Bridge south to Key West is known as the **Lower Keys**. This is what people dream of when they think of the Keys: peace and quiet, stunning views and undisturbed wildlife. Parks include the **Bahia Honda State Park** with cabins and camp sites overlooking the ocean, the **Looe Key National Marine**

Sanctuary named after the HMS *Looe* which ran aground here in 1744, and the **Key Deer National Wildlife Refuge**, which is home to several hundred miniature deer. A subspecies of the Virginia white-tailed deer, this little animal has been under threat from encroaching human development and traffic on the main highway.

Above: *The strange Ripley's Believe It or Not! in Duval Street, Key West.*
Opposite: *Catch of the day – a huge marlin caught off the Florida Keys.*

Key West ★★★

Key West has become a legend in its own lifetime, a place people visit to experience something different. Once a barely accessible paradise for escapists, Key West has since been forced into the mainstream by hordes of tourists yet retains some of the quirkiness that makes it so unique.

In April 1982 the United States Border Patrol set up roadblocks across the Overseas Highway just south of Florida City in an attempt to stem the flow of illegal aliens from here into the United States. Traffic chaos ensued as police searched every vehicle, demanding occupants produce proof of their US citizenship. In protest at being treated like foreigners in their own country, city officials of Key West proclaimed the **Conch Republic**, complete with separate flag, mock visas, border passes and currency, forcing a chagrined border patrol to beat a hasty retreat. 'Conch' passports and visas are still available from the Key West Chamber of Commerce and the Conch Republic Celebration, in honour of the 'secessionists victory', is held in April every year.

Always out on a limb, the Key West inhabitants started out as **wreckers**, aiding the victims of shipwrecks and rescuing cargo, though stories of deliberate wrecking abound.

Its uniqueness has subsequently appealed to eccentrics and celebrities. The committed environmentalist **John Audubon** started preservation awareness and helped retain much of the history of the island. **Ernest Hemingway** found inspiration for much of his work while living here.

Key West is hedonism at its best. In the evening, head down **Duval Street** to festive **Mallory Square**, where locals and tourists mingle with jugglers, fire eaters and buskers, as the sun sets to a round of applause. Mallory Square forms the starting point for lively evenings out in the many bars, cafés and restaurants, most of which have excellent live music with a Caribbean flavour.

During the day, a good place to start a tour is on Truman Avenue. Turn left on Lean Street to find the home of playwright **Tennessee Williams**. Continue down

---

END OF THE ROAD

The cluster of islands lying beyond Key West is called the **Dry Tortugas**. Known as the Gibraltar of the Gulf due to their strategic position, they were of prime military importance in the past. Fort Jefferson on Garden Key has artillery tiers for 450 guns and 50ft (15m) walls 8ft (2½m) thick. Used as a prison after the Civil War, it is now a tourist site.

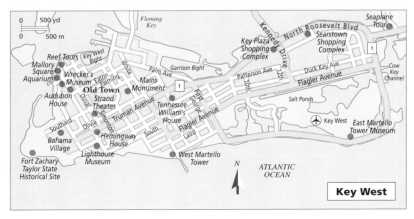

Key West

Truman Avenue and turn left into **Whitehead Street** to
reach the most southerly point of mainland America
accessible to the public. Turn right to find the **Lighthouse
Museum** where you can climb 98 steps for lovely views
across the island and out to sea.

Almost opposite is the unusual **Hemingway House**
(open 09:00–17:00 daily). Dating back to 1851, this was
the famous author's home until his death in 1961. It was
the first house in Key West to have running water, a fire-
place and a pool. The headboard of the bed is made from
a 17th-century Spanish monastery gate, the glass chan-
delier was hand-blown and the Picasso cat was a gift to
the author from Pablo Picasso himself. The house is now
a museum and inhabited by 42 cats (most with six toes
or more), one for each bridge in the Keys.

Left off Whitehead and into Petronia Street, you reach
the lively Caribbean-style **Bahama Village** neighbourhood. Further north, at the corner of Whitehead Street
and **Greene Street**, among a row of irresistibly quaint
'gingerbread' conch-style houses, is **John Audubon**'s
residence, filled with a priceless collection of furniture
from the mid-1800s and original bird engravings by the
artist. Open 09:30–17:00 daily.

Opposite is the **Mel Fisher Maritime Heritage
Society Museum**, housing treasure that was lost by two
Spanish galleons which foundered during a hurricane in
1622. Just down the road, back on Duval Street, is the
Wrecker's Museum, built
in 1829 for Florida Senator
Watlington, who was also
a sea captain and wrecker.
The house is said to be the
oldest in Key West.

The delightful pink and
green house at the end of
the street is often called the
Southernmost House. This
is actually a misnomer,
since another one was
erected just south of it.

HEMINGWAY DAYS

Ernest 'Papa' Hemingway
wrote *For Whom the Bell
Tolls*, *The Green Hills of
Africa*, *A Farewell to Arms*,
The Snows of Kilimanjaro,
Death in the Afternoon and
The Old Man and the Sea
while living on Whitehead
Street in Key West, between
organizing boxing matches
and drinking at Sloppy Joe's.

Opposite: *Famous author,
Ernest Hemingway, accessed
his study via a catwalk.*
Below: *Aerial view of Fort
Jefferson (Dry Tortugas).*

The Florida Keys at a Glance

The climate is kinder in the Keys than on the mainland. **Summer** temperatures reach 80°F (27°C) in July and drop to around 70°F (21°C) in the winter. Winds keep the islands **free of humidity** in summer and warm in winter. **Hurricane** season extends from **August** to **October** and tropical storms occur through-out the summer months. The Keys are busy in winter, but limited accommodation keeps tourist numbers to manageable levels.

Key West International Airport is on the southeast corner of the island, while the new **Marathon Airport** is on Marathon at MM52. Direct international flights into the Keys are not available and most visitors use Miami as a gateway – flying time is 45 minutes to Key West and 35 minutes to Marathon. The majority of visitors arrive by car. The only road to the Keys is **Highway 1** (the Over-seas Highway), which heads south out of Florida City and continues down to Key West across 43 bridges. This road is marked per mile, directions are given by **Mile Marker** (MM) with MM1 on the tip of Key West. There is no train service, since the line was destroyed by a hurricane in the 1930s, but you can arrive by yacht or cruise line.

Most of the islands are small enough to explore on foot, but taxis are available. Key West has two tourist services, known as: **Conch Tour Train**, tel: (305) 294-5161 and **Old Town Trolley**, 1910 N Roosevelt Blvd, tel: (305) 296-6688. Both of these take about 90 minutes to tour the town.

You should book ahead for any establishment in the Keys. The relatively few hotels are extremely popular, particularly around Christmas, in the summer season and on United States holiday weekends.

Key Largo
LUXURY
Holiday Inn Key Largo Resort and Marina, 99701 Overseas Highway, tel: (305) 451-1133, fax: 451-2955. Renovated by the man who also restored the *African Queen*, moored outside.
Jules Verne Undersea Lodge, 51 Shoreland Drive, tel 1-800 858-7119. A 600ft^2 lodge anchored 30ft (9m) under water. Booked up more than a year ahead but not cheap.

MID-RANGE
Marina del Mar Resort and Marina, 527 Caribbean Drive, Key Largo, tel: (305) 451-3483, fax: 451-4107.

Ocean Point Suites, 500 Burton Drive, Key Largo, tel: (305) 853-3000.

Islamorada
LUXURY
Checca Lodge, MM82, Upper Matecumbe Key, tel: (305) 664-4651, fax: 664-2083. Won awards for its environmentally friendly schemes. Calm and spacious.

MID-RANGE
Breezy Palms Resort, PO Box 767, tel: (305) 664-2361.
Pelican Cove, 84457 Old Overseas Highway, tel: (305) 664-2361.

Marathon
LUXURY
Hawk's Cay Resort, tel: (305) 743-9018.
Faro Blanco Marine Resort, tel: (305) 743-9018.

MID-RANGE
Banana Bay Resort and Marina, 4590 Overseas Highway, tel: (305) 743-3500, fax: 743-2670. A beautiful and very relaxing resort.
Sombero Resort and Lighthouse Marina, 19 Sombero Beach Blvd, tel: (305) 289-1478, fax: 743-2998. Suites all have kitchens, good marina.

BUDGET
Seascape Oceanfront Resort, tel: (305) 743-6455.
Howard Johnson Resort, tel: (305) 743-8550.

The Florida Keys at a Glance

Key West
LUXURY
The Banyan Resort, 323
Whitehead St, tel: (305)
296-7786, fax: 294-1107.
Within walking distance
of Old Town attractions,
it has pleasant gardens.
Holiday Inn La Concha, 430
Duval St, tel: (305) 296-2991,
fax: 294-3283. Seven storeys
of Art Deco; guests have
included Ernest Hemingway
and Tennessee Williams.
Fairfield Inn, 2400
N Roosevelt Blvd, tel: (305)
296-5700, fax: 292-9840.
Free breakfast, two pools and
only a mile from downtown.

WHERE TO EAT

The Keys have their very own
cuisine with an emphasis on
seafood. Eat stone crabs in
season (15 October–15 May),
when they can legally be
harvested – and definitely
sample some Key lime pie.

Key Largo
Mrs Mac's Kitchen,
MM99, tel: (305) 451-3722.
Very good food and lovely
international decor.

Islamorada
Marker 88,
tel: (305) 852-9315. Casual
but costly, award-winning
food in a tropical setting.

Marathon
Grassy Key Dairy Bar,
MM58.5, tel: (305) 743-3816.
Good food at good prices.

Kelsey's, M48, 1996
Overseas Highway, Docks of
Faro Blanco Resort, tel: (305)
743-9018. Beautiful setting,
overlooking the ocean,
local dishes a speciality.

Key West
**Pepe's Cafe and Steak
House**, 806 Caroline St,
tel: (305) 294-7192.
The best place in town for
breakfast; meet the locals in
this small shack which serves
affordable meals all day long.
Half Shell Raw Bar,
Land's End Marina, tel: (305)
294-7496. Huge plates of
oysters and conch chowder
are two of the best dishes.
Sloppy Joe's, 201 Duval St,
tel: (305) 294-5717. Former
haunt of Ernest Hemingway,
now a tourist trap but still
a definite 'must see'.

SHOPPING

Not much exciting shopping is
to be had in the Keys, beyond
the normal resort shops, and
souvenir T-shirt stalls.

Mallory Square, Key West
is the main centre, tel:
(305) 296-4557.

The Rain Barrel,
Islamorada. Art show in
March, with 100 artists
and some 20,000 visitors.
Fast Buck Freddie's,
500 Duval St. A Greenpeace
outpost selling rather offbeat
items like Pelican Poop.

TOURS AND EXCURSIONS

Fort Jefferson Ferry,
tel: (305) 294-7009. Day trips
to the offshore monument.
Old Town Trolley Tours,
1910 N Roosevelt Blvd, Key
West, tel: (305) 296-6688.
90-minute tour of attractions
with 12 stops along the way.
Conch Tour Train, Key Lime
Square, Key West, tel: (305)
294-5161. 90-minute tours.

USEFUL CONTACTS

**Florida Keys and Key West
Visitor 's Bureau**, POBox
866, Key West, FL 33041-
0866, tel: (305) 296-1552.
**Key West Reservation
Service**, 628 Fleming St, tel:
(305) 294-8850, fax: 296-
6291. For accommodation.
**Coast Guard Group Key
West**, tel: (305) 292-8727.
Information on navigational
hazards, safety and weather.

KEY WEST	J	F	M	A	M	J	J	A	S	O	N	D
AVERAGE TEMP. °F	65	67	68	72	74	77	79	79	77	76	70	67
AVERAGE TEMP. °C	18	19	20	22	23	25	26	26	25	24	21	19
HOURS OF SUN DAILY	12	12	12	13	13	14	14	14	13	12	12	12
RAINFALL in	2	2	2	3	6.5	9	6	7	8	7	2.5	2
RAINFALL mm	51	51	51	76	165	229	152	179	203	179	63	51
DAYS OF RAINFALL	7	7	7	8	12	15	13	13	14	13	8	7

Travel Tips

Tourist Information

The Florida Tourism Industry Marketing Corporation has branches in Frankfurt, Tokyo, Sao Paulo, and Toronto. The **London** address is: 18/24 Westbourne Grove, London W2 5RH, tel: (0171) 792-0087. The head office is in: **Tallahassee**, 107 W Gaines St, Suite 566, FL32399-2000, tel: (904) 488-7598, fax: 487-0134. Each county and city has its own separate tourism office. Greater **Miami** Convention and Visitors Bureau, tel: (305) 539-3000. Greater **Fort Lauderdale** Convention and Visitors Bureau, tel: (305) 765-4466. **Tampa–Hillsborough** Convention and Visitors Bureau, tel: (813) 223-2752. **St Petersburg–Clearwater** Area Convention and Visitors Bureau, tel: (813) 582-7892. **Orlando–Orange County** Convention and Visitors Bureau, tel: (407) 363-5892. **Kissimmee–St Cloud** Convention and Visitors **Bureau**, tel: (407) 847-5000. **Daytona Beach Area** Convention and Visitors Bureau, tel: (904) 255-0415.

Jacksonville and the Beaches Convention and Visitors Bureau, tel: (904) 798-9148. Information about attractions can be obtained from **Florida Attractions Association**, Box 10295, Tallahassee FL32302, tel: (904) 222-2885. Information about state parks and recreation areas comes from **Office of Recreation and Parks**, Mail Station 535, 3900 Commonwealth Blvd, Tallahassee, FL32399-3000, tel: (904) 488-9872.

Entry Requirements

Visitors must be in possession of a valid passport and be able to show a return air ticket. European Union citizens may enter the United States under the visa waiver scheme and will be given the necessary forms as they enter the country. Anyone staying longer than 90 days must have a visa. Citizens other than those from Britain, New Zealand, Japan and most western European countries need a valid passport that expires at least six months after their visit to the United States has ended. Multiple re-entry visas are valid for 10 years and can be transferred to new passports. Visa costs vary according to nationality. Those with multiple re-entry visas will be able to enter blue lanes at immigration points, which should be quicker. In Britain, visas can be obtained in writing from the **Visa and Immigration Dept of the United States**, United States Embassy, 5 Upper Grosvenor St, London W1A 2JB, tel: (0171) 499-3443.

Customs

Customs forms have to be completed before arrival. Familiar red and green channels greet visitors at the airport. Allowances for nonresident adults (over 21) are: 1 litre spirits, 200 cigarettes or 50 cigars or 2 kilograms of tobacco, and 100ml of perfume. Unlicensed importation of fruit, plants and meat is banned – travel snacks like apples will be confiscated.

Health Requirements

No vaccinations are required to enter the United States, unless coming from an area suffering from outbreaks of cholera or yellow fever.

However, adequate health insurance cover is essential. Florida has a very good health and dental care system but it is extremely expensive. Carry a doctor's prescription to allay fears of drug smuggling if you are on medication involving narcotics or syringes.

Getting There

By Air: All main US carriers fly into Florida. The major gateways from Europe are Miami International Airport and Orlando International Airport, although an increasing amount of traffic is handled by Tampa. St Petersburg International Airport receives charter flights from Europe. All the bigger cities have regional airports with extensive connections from the main entry points into Florida and from other parts of the United States.
By Road: The network of the efficient Greyhound bus service extends all over the United States and into Florida.
By Rail: Amtrak operates a national service, though not all areas in Florida are connected. The main railway line runs down to Miami but bypasses some of the central east coast. There are no links through the Everglades or into the Keys.
By Boat: With so many thousands of kilometres of coastline, Florida has a large variety of ports, marinas and docks. Most major cruise lines regularly dock in a Florida port, and yacht charters are available to and from the region. An abundance of ferry services operate from mainland destinations to the offshore barrier islands.

What to Pack

Florida, generally, is very casual. Pack according to season. Take a jumper in winter, particularly if you are visiting the north of the state. In summer, pack light, loose clothing appropriate for humid weather, but be prepared for tropical rainstorms. You'll need plenty of sun cream and don't forget súnglasses and a hat. Comfortable shoes are a necessity for theme parks, which usually require a lot of walking and queueing. In summer, mosquitoes and other biting bugs are rampant, so take enough repellent. Don't worry if you do forget something; it will be available across the state, probably at less cost than at home.

Money Matters

Currency: The official currency is the dollar, symbolized by the $ sign. One dollar is divided into 100 cents in the following denominations: 5 cents (nickel), 10 cents (dime) and 25 cents (quarter). Avoid carrying large sums in cash with you and consider taking United States currency traveller's cheques. Note that cheques in pound sterling and other European currencies will not be changed except at the bigger banks. Major credit cards are widely accepted and most Americans use plastic rather than cash.
Exchange: Foreign exchange desks are located at airports, banks and most hotels. Banks are generally open 10:00–15:00 Monday–Thursday, and 10:00–17:00 on Friday. Car hire companies and hotels may require a credit card

SEASONAL EVENTS

Mid-January •
Art Deco Weekend,
Miami South Beach.
February •
Daytona Speed Weeks.
February •
Florida Strawberry Festival,
Plant City.
February •
Olustee Battle Festival,
Lake City (Civil War battle
re-enactment in the country).
Early March • Carnaval
Miami, Little Havana.
Mid-July •
Hemingway Days Festival,
Key West.
Early September •
Founding of St Augustine.

swipe before handing over a vehicle or checking you in.
Tipping: Most restaurants and bars add a 15% service charge to your bill, but an additional tip is expected for good service. Taxi drivers expect at least 10 per cent in tips, and airport and hotel porters demand a minimum of US$1 per bag.
Sales tax: The six per cent is not usually included in the displayed price, and will be added to the bill at the check out.

Accommodation

Florida offers an enormous choice of accommodation. Peak season varies from north to south but, generally speaking, if you plan to be in the south in winter or in the north in summer, book ahead. Accommodation varies from inexpensive motels to high-rise tourist hotels. Luxury resorts are often low-rise and spread over hundreds of acres.

City-centre hotels and those near the major airports tend to cater for business travellers and are priced accordingly. All the major American hotel chains are well represented in the state and will book you into other chain members elsewhere on request.

If travelling alone, watch out for singles' supplements, which can almost double the cost of a room.

Most reservations are kept open until 17:00 or 18:00, but this can be extended if the hotel is warned in advance of your late arrival. Most establishments will require at least one night's payment in advance, or a tour operator voucher or proof of payment. Do not commit yourself unnecessarily to half-board or even bed and breakfast – eating out is so cheap, that many hotels quote a simple room rate knowing guests prefer to eat elsewhere.

Eating Out

Florida prides itself on its fresh seafood and freshly grown fruits and vegetables. Portions are large and prices generally low. Meals can be true feasts, with pancakes and massive omelettes for breakfast, and eat-as-much-as-you-can buffets in the evening.

On Sunday, breakfast and lunch will often be merged into brunch, a massive banquet, frequently served with a glass of champagne, orange juice or a Bloody Mary.

It is interesting to note the regional differences within the state. To the north the food is influenced by Southern cooking and Creole cuisine. Grits, okra (a long, thin vegetable), fried aubergine (eggplant), fried chicken and corn bread are among the staples. Further south the cooking is more than a little influenced by 20th-century immigrants. Spicy Cuban and Caribbean foods are commonplace in Miami, where Spanish style also abounds. Alligator appears on menus seasonally: try it, it tastes a bit like chicken, and is reassuringly eco-friendly, coming from a well-orchestrated culling programme that keeps the numbers balanced. In the Keys, the food is slightly different again – there is much more delectable seafood on offer and, of course, tasty Key lime pie for dessert.

Transport

Air: All major US carriers fly into Florida, while American Eagle, Delta and USAir all offer comprehensive networks within Florida. The air passes of some airlines cost much the same as bus or rail tickets, a good bargain.

Road: Road networks are good, with major and inter-state highways (motorways) running north to south and east to west. There are a few toll roads. Most towns and cities are laid out on a grid system, many based on numbered streets, which usually run in one direction only, with avenues or boulevards intersecting at 90-degree angles. All car rental companies have outlets in the major centres and at airports, but shop around for the best deal. Fly-drive packages often present the cheapest and easiest way of arranging a car. Anyone over 16, with a valid driving licence, can drive in Florida, though most rental companies insist that drivers be over 25. Insurance may be arranged by the car hire firm.

Road Rules: Driving is on the right. Rectangular green road signs usually provide directions, while yellow signs contain safety information. White signs show speed limits: 15mph (24kph) in school zones, 25mph (40kph) on residential streets and between 35–55mph (56–88kph) on main streets.

CONVERSION CHART		
FROM	TO	MULTIPLY BY
Millimetres	Inches	0.0394
Metres	Yards	1.0936
Metres	Feet	3.281
Kilometres	Miles	0.6214
Kilometres square	Square miles	0.386
Hectares	Acres	2.471
Litres	Pints	1.760
Kilograms	Pounds	2.205
Tonnes	Tons	0.984
To convert Celsius to Fahrenheit: x 9 ÷ 5 + 32		

Interstate highways are usually 55mph (90kph) in towns and 65mph (105kph) in rural areas. All front seat passengers must wear seat belts. Children under three must sit in approved car seats, which rental companies can usually supply. You should drive with headlights on if it rains hard enough to have to use windshield wipers. Florida's anti-drink-drive laws are tough: offenders face heavy fines and possible jail terms. If you park unlawfully or overstay your metered time, your vehicle will be towed away. Parking within three metres of a fire hydrant is viewed as an offence. Try to park in the shade, as cars can get too hot to touch in the full summer sun, which is why it is illegal to leave animals in parked cars.

Buses: Local networks mostly run on routes planned for residents and commuters rather than tourists, and serve cities, counties or beach areas. Check route and times before tackling local services – most require an exact fare. Greyhound operates interstate and serves the major cities. Cities like Miami have buses arriving almost hourly; others only have daily or weekly services, so check ahead and plan carefully.

Rail: Railway services are not so good in Florida. Amtrak never offers more than two services a day to any city and prices are not low enough to be attractive. Rail passes, bought before leaving home, can cut the cost. Travel agents in Europe sell both Greyhound and Amtrak tickets and can book you on specified services.

Business hours

Most shopping malls are open 10:00–21:00 Monday–Saturday, and 10:00–18:00 on Sunday. Other shops and offices generally open 09:00–17:00 Monday–Saturday.

Time Difference

Florida has two time zones. Most of the state operates on Eastern Standard Time while the northwest region, west of the Apalachicola River, operates on Central Standard Time. Eastern Standard Time is five hours behind Greenwich Mean (or Universal Standard) Time (GMT) in winter, while Central Standard Time is six hours behind. Florida has United States Daylight Saving Time, advancing clocks by one hour from the last Sunday in April to the last Sunday in October.

Communications

Postal services are generally very efficient. Stamps can be bought (at a small extra cost) from hotels and vending machines or at post offices. Post offices are open 09:00–17:00 Monday to Friday, and 09:00–noon on Saturday. Post your letters in blue mailboxes on the street, in post offices or hotel lobbies. Mail to Europe takes about one week to arrive.

The international telephone dialling code for the United States is 1. Florida has seven telephone area codes: 305 for Dade County, the Keys and Key West; 954 for Broward County; 407 from Boca Raton/Palm Beach north through central Florida; 813

for the central west; 941 for the southwest; 904 for northwest and northeast; and 352 for the western Big Bend area and inland.

Most hotels have direct dial telephones for international calls to Europe, although a credit card imprint may be required before you are allowed to use one.

Public telephones are cheaper and can be found on street corners, at bars, restaurants, hotel lobbies, bus and rail stations. An automated voice will ask you to insert coins when required. The phone may ring immediately after you finish a call to request more money. If you do not comply, the person you called will be billed. Nonlocal and long-distance calls are cheaper between 18:00–08:00. International calls are cheapest between 23:00–07:00. Many tourist agencies, theme parks, attractions and car hire firms have a toll-free number (prefix 800), which can only be accessed from inside the United States.

Electricity

The electricity circuit runs on 110 volts, which means that equipment from many European and other countries will not work without an adaptor. The American plugs are two-pronged, but since some adaptors don't fit the United States sockets you are advised to check when buying.

Weights and Measures

All measures are imperial rather than metric in the United States. Petrol is bought in United States gallons, which are slightly smaller than the European gallon. Clothing sizes are smaller – buy a United States size 10 if you would normally wear a European size 12. For shoes, add one to the measurement (i.e. try on a size five when you would normally wear a size four).

Health precautions

Florida is a safe and healthy place. Water is safe to drink and food hygiene standards generally excellent. The sun is strong, so take sun cream, hats and sunglasses to avoid sunburn. If on medication,

take sufficient with you – it will be available but may be more costly in Florida.

Health Services

Health services throughout Florida are comprehensive but expensive. Make sure you are properly insured, including sufficient for repatriation if necessary. Hotels usually have a doctor on call 24 hours a day.

Personal Safety

Tourism suffered in 1994, after a few fatal incidents involving tourists. The state reacted fast and set up several help schemes designed to clamp down on crime. The situation has greatly improved, but a few basic guidelines remain:
• Do not carry large sums of cash or wear a lot of jewellery around town, at theme parks and other attractions.
• Do not walk around the city streets at night.
• Always check parking lots for suspicious characters before leaving your car.
• Park in well-lit areas only.
• Ask for directions before leaving the hotel or airport.
• If you get lost, find a well-lit petrol station or public building to ask for assistance.
• Some rental companies offer mobile phones for use in emergencies – use them.
• If you are bumped from behind while driving, do not stop. Drive somewhere safe, then call the police if necessary.
• Do not open your hotel room door without checking to see who it is first.
• Do not take valuables to the beach with you.

• In any emergency call **911**. The police have multilingual staff working on help lines with tourist advice.

Emergencies

The **police**, **ambulance** and **fire service** can be contacted by dialling **911**.
Companies issuing traveller's cheques may be reached on toll-free numbers in the United States. You are advised to keep this number separate from your cheques and call immediately if you have lost your cheques or had them stolen. The British Consulate has an office in Miami, tel: (305) 374-1522, which you should contact if you lose your passport. Also, report stolen or lost passports or traveller's cheques to the police.

Etiquette

Florida is a friendly place with a relaxed ambience. Dress codes are usually equally relaxed – in the evenings, however, you may want to cover up.

GOOD READING

• Brogan, Hugh (1990) *The Penguin History of the United States of America*. Penguin.
• Bryson, Bill (1996) *Made in America*. Minerva.
• Carr, Archie Fairly (1955) *Guide to the Reptiles, Amphibians and Freshwater Fishes of Florida*. FUP.
• Rawlings, Marjorie Kinnan (1992) *The Yearling*. Mammoth.
• Hemingway, Ernest (1976) *The Old Man and the Sea*. Triad; (1990) *Islands in the Stream*. Grafton.

INDEX

Note: Numbers in bold indicate photographs

African Queen 114
Al Capone 16, 35
alligators 9, 37, 79, 84
Amelia Island 79, 83, 87
American Civil War 14, 85, 90
Anna Maria Island **106**, 107
Apalachicola 13–14, 96
National Forest 8, 96, **97**
Arthur R Marshall Loxahatchee National Wildlife Refuge 42
Astronaut Memorial Planetarium and Observatory **66**, 67
Audubon, John 118, 119

Bahia Honda State Park 117
Bailey-Matthews Shell Museum 108
Battle of Natural Bridge 23, 89, 94
Battle of Olustee 15, 23
beaches 66, 101
Amelia Island 79
Atlantic 82
Bahia Honda **7**
Daytona 5
Destin 92
Fort Myers **109**
Fort Walton **92**
Jacksonville 82
Madeira Beach 105
Neptune 82
Panama City 89
Ponte Vedra 82
Sanibel Island 108
South Beach Miami 5
St Augustine 82
St Petersburg 5, **104**
Tigertail **102**
Bethune, Mary McLeod 72
birds **9**, 37, 66, 70, 75, 92, 97, 105, 109
Blue Springs State Park 75
Boca Grande 109
Boca Raton 40
Bok Tower Gardens 59
Bradenton 106
Manatee Village Historical Park 106
Bulow Plantation Ruins State Historic Site 75

Cabbage Key 109
Campbell, Sir Malcolm 63, 71, 73
Cape Canaveral 16, 67–68
Captiva Island 109
Castro, Fidel 16, 21
Cedar Key 89, 97
Christ of the Deep 115
citrus farming **8**, **14**, 18, 28, **65**
Clearwater 105, 110
Clermont 56
climate 7, 26
Cocoa Beach 63, **67**
Conservancy's Naples Nature Center 109
Corkscrew Swamp Sanctuary 101, 109
Crocodile Lakes National Wildlife Refuge 114
crocodiles 9, 36, **37**
Cubans 16, **20**, 21, 28, 33, 102
Cypress Gardens **58**, **59**

Daytona Beach 24, 63, 71–73
Speedway 63, 70, 73, **74**
Interactive Motor Sports Center 74
watchtower **72**
DeLand 75
De León Springs National Park **75**
de Luna y Arellano, Tristan 11
de Narváez, Panfilo 11
De Soto Archaeological Site 96
de Soto, Hernando 102
Devil's Millhopper State Geological Site 85
Drake, Sir Francis 12
Dry Tortugas 6, 8, 113, 118
Fort Jefferson **119**
Dunedin 104

Edison, Thomas 108
Eglin Air Force Base 91
Egmont Key 107
Emerald Coast 6, **93**
Everglades National Park 5, **6**, 8, 9, 14, **19**, 25, **36**, 37, 45
Billie Swamp Safari 27, 38
Corkscrew Swamp Sanctuary 37

Fernandina Beach 79
festivals 23, 71, 74, 79, 123
Firestone, Harvey 73
fish 9, 75, 103
Fisher, Mel 43, 119
Flagler, Henry Morrison **15**, 32, 40
flora 6, 8, 36, 70, 85, 96, 108
Florida Caverns State Park 89, 96
Florida Keys 24, 113–121
Marine Sanctuary 113
food 28–29
Ford, Henry 73, 108
Forest Capital State Museum 97
Fort Caroline National Memorial 83
Fort Clinch State Park 83
Fort Lauderdale 31, 38–39
Bonnet House 39
Butterfly World 38
Flamingo Gardens 38
IMAX Theater 39
International Swimming Hall of Fame 25, 39
Las Olas Boulevard 38–39
promenade **38**
Stranahan House 39
Fort Myers 10, 101
Historical Museum 108
Fort Pierce 43
SEAL Museum 22

Gainesville 84–85
Harn Museum **84**
Kanapaha Botanical Gardens 84
Gamble, Major Robert 106
Gasparilla Island 109
Geronimo, Chief 15, 90
golf **25**, 64
Gorrie, John 14
government 17–18
Grassy Key Dolphin Research Center 113
Gulf of Mexico 6

Halifax River 71
Hemingway, Ernest 113, 119
Hibiscus Island 35
Hickory Mound Impoundment 97
history 10–16, 23, 84
hurricanes 7, 11, 15, 89

Indian Key 117
Indian Shores, Suncoast Seabird Sanctuary 105
Islamorada 115

Jackson, General Andrew 13, 90
Jacksonville 5, 23, **82**, 83
brewing industry 82, **83**
Florida Theater 82
Landing 83
River City Playhouse 82
Riverwalk 79, 83
JN 'Ding' Darling National Wildlife Refuge 108, 109
John F Kennedy Space Center 5, **16**, 26, **69**
Rocket Park 62
John Pennekamp Coral Reef Marine Park 5, 8, 113, **114**
John's Pass **27**, **28**, 105
Jupiter 42

Kennedy, John F 67
Key Biscayne 24
Key Deer National Wildlife Refuge 117
Key Largo 113–114
Key lime pie 28, 29, 121
Key West 5, **24**, 117
Bahama Village 119
Hemingway Festival 23
Hemingway House **118**
Mallory Square 113, 118
Sunset Pier 20
Wrecker's Museum 113
Kissimmee 47, 57–58
Fighter Pilots USA 58
World of Orchids 58
Klassix Auto Museum 74

Lake County 47, 54–55
Lake Okeechobee 6, 42
Lake Tohopekaliga 57, 59
Lake Wales Amphitheater 59
Lake Woodruff National Wildlife Refuge 75
Lignumvitae Key 116
Long Key State Recreation Area 115
Longboat Key 107
Looe Key National Marine Sanctuary 117

manatee **9**, 36, 66, 75, 97, 103, 106
Marathon 116

Marco Island 108–109
Marjorie Kinnan Rawlings
  State Historical Site 79, **85**
Martin County 31, 42–43
Masaryktown 104
Matecumba Key **115**
Melbourne 66
Menéndez de Avilés,
  Pedro 11
Merritt Island National
  Wildlife Refuge 63, 69, 77
Miami 15, 32–35
  American Police
    Hall of Fame 22
  Art Deco District 16, 29,
    34, **35**
  Art Deco Weekend 23
  Bayside Marketplace 32
  Biltmore Hotel **33**
  Calle Ocho 21
  Carnaval Miami 23
  Coconut Grove 33
  Coral Gables 33
  Henry Morrison Flagler
    Museum 27
  Jewish Memorial 22
  Jungle Queen 27
  Little Havana 21, 33
  Metromover 32
  Miami Beach **30**, 34, **35**
  Miracle Mile 33
  port **18**
  South Beach (SoBe) 5, 31
Micanopy 85
Mizner, Addison 40
Mount Dora 55
Myakka River State Park
  106

Naples 101, 109
NASA 16, 67
native Americans **19**
  Calusa **10**, 11, 14
  Creek 14
  Miccosukee 37
  Muskogee 14
  Seminole 13, 14, 19,
    27, 39, 75
  Tequesta 14
  Timucua 73, 85, 106
New Smyrna **70**
North Hill Preservation
  District *see* Pensacola

Ocala 47
  National Forest 8, 55, 56
  Silver Springs **54**
  Wild Waters 56
Orlando 48–49

Orlando cont.
  Church Street Station
    29, 47, 49
  Gatorland 26, **57**
  Harry P Leu Botanical
    Gardens 49
  Mystery Fun House 52
  Sea World 26, **53**
  Wet 'n Wild 26, **46**, 53
  Wilderness Park 54
  Winter Park 47, **49**
Ormond Beach 73
Osceola National Forest 8
Overseas Highway
  18, 113, 115

Palm Beach **25**, 31, 40–41
  Whitehall **40**
  Worth Avenue 41
Palm Beach County 40–41
Palm Island 35
Panama City 92–93
  Gulf World 92
  Miracle Strip Amusement
    Park 93
  Museum of Man
    in the Sea **93**
  Shipwreck Island
    Water Park 93
  Zoo World 93
Panhandle 6, **88**, 89
panther 9, 36
Parker Manatee Aquarium
  106
Peacock Springs State
  Recreation Area 5
Pensacola 5, 11, 13,
  22, 89–91
  National Museum of
    Naval Aviation 27,
    89, **91**
North Hill Preservation
  District 89
  Three Mile Bridge 91
Perdido Key 92
Pinellas Peninsula 105
Plant, Henry 101
Polk County 47, 59
polo **41**
Ponce de León Inlet
  Lighthouse **73**
Ponce de León, Juan **11**
Ponte Vedra 86

Ringling, John 21
  Museum of Art 22, 107
  Circus Museum 22
Ripley's Believe It or Not!
  53, 81, **117**

Sanibel Island **108**, 109
Sarasota 21, 101, 107
  Asolo Performing Arts
    Center 22, 107
  Bellm's Cars and Music
    of Yesteryear 107
  Ca'd'Zan 107
Sebastian Inlet State
  Recreation Area 65
Sebring 24
Seminole Wars 13
Seven Mile Bridge 113
Siesta Key 107
shopping **27**
slavery 20, 95
Space Coast 63, 67
St Andrews State Area 93
St Armands Key 107
St Augustine 5, 10, 13,
  22, 78, 80–81
  Alligator Farm 79, 81
  Basilica Cathedral of
    St Augustine 81
  Castillo de San Marcos
    12, 13, 80
  Lightner Museum 81
  Mission of Nombre
    de Dios 81
  National Archaeological
    Park 81
  Oldest
    House 81
    Store Museum **80**, 81
    Wooden Schoolhouse
      80, **81**
  Potter's Wax Museum
    27, 81
  Spanish Quarter 79–80
St Cloud
  Reptile World
    Serpentarium 57
  Silver Spurs Rodeo 47
  Water Mania 58
St Lucie Inlet State
  Preserve 43
St Marks **96**
St Petersburg 101
  Beach **104**
  Sunken Gardens 105
Stuart 31
  Elliott Museum **42**
  Gilbert's Bar House
    of Refuge 42

Tallahassee 5, 13, 89
  New Capitol 94
  Old Capitol **94**
  Senate House 17
  Supreme Court **95**

Tampa Bay 22, 101–103
  Adventure Island
    26, 103
  Buccaneer Bay 103
  Busch Gardens
    5, 26, 101, **103**
  Florida Aquarium
    103, 105
  Garrison Seaport Center
    103, 105
  Lowry Park Zoo 103
  Old Hyde Park Village 102
  Performing Arts Center 22
  Ybor City **23**, 29,
    101–102, **103**
Tarpon Springs 104
Tavernier 114
Titusville 63
  Enchanted Forest 69
Tomoka State Park 73
Torreya State Park 89, 96
Tosohatchee State
  Reserve 54
Treasure Coast 43, 63
turtles 9, 68, 75, 105

United States Air Force
  Armament Museum 91
Universal Studios 5, 47, **52**
US Astronaut Hall of Fame
  26, 63, **68**
US Space Camp Florida 69

Venice 101
Vero Beach 64–65
  McKee Botanical Gardens
    65

Wakulla Springs 97, 99
Walt Disney World
  5, 26–27, 50–51
  Disney–MGM Studios 51
  Epcot 47, **50**, 51
  Magic Kingdom
    47, 50–51
watersports 24, **93, 112**,
Watson Island 35
Wekiwa Springs
  State Park 54
West Palm Beach 41
  Dreher Park Zoo 41
  Kravis Cultural Center
    22, 41
  Norton Gallery of Art 41
Williams, Tennessee
Windley Key 115

Ybor, Don Vincente
  Martinez 102